HOPSCOTCH

...or why children are the better day traders

A Modern Guide to Direct-Access Trading

By Matthias Thoma

www.hopscotch.cc

National Library of Canada Cataloguing in Publication Data

Thoma, Matthias, 1968-
         Hopscotch-- or why children are the better day
traders / Matthias Thoma.
ISBN 1-4120-0251-6
         1. Investments. 2. Finance, Personal. I. Title
HG4521.T46 2003   332.024'01
C2003-902176-9

TRAFFORD

This book was published *on-demand* in cooperation with Trafford Publishing. On-demand publishing is a unique process and service of making a book available for retail sale to the public taking advantage of on-demand manufacturing and Internet marketing. **On-demand publishing** includes promotions, retail sales, manufacturing, order fulfilment, accounting and collecting royalties on behalf of the author.

Suite 6E, 2333 Government St., Victoria, B.C. V8T 4P4, CANADA

Phone	250-383-6864	Toll-free	1-888-232-4444 (Canada & US)
Fax	250-383-6804	E-mail	sales@trafford.com
Web site	www.trafford.com	TRAFFORD PUBLISHING IS A DIVISION OF TRAFFORD HOLDINGS LTD.	
Trafford Catalogue #03-0620		www.trafford.com/robots/03-0620.html	

10   9   8   7   6   5   4   3   2

Index

Prologue

Many books have been written about the subject of day-trading, or as it is now called direct access trading. However, as with many situations in life it helps sometimes to look at things from a new angle. Other, no doubt revered, authors have created 200, sometimes even 300 page monster books about trading. I honestly believe if one can not bring a successful strategy across with a concise description, it is probably far too difficult to actually apply it in real market conditions. Please do not confuse mass with quality. This comparably small book is well worth the investment. Please feel free to contact me with concerns, comments or follow up questions. Please visit www.hopsctoch.cc to find out how to reach me.

This book gives you an introduction to direct access trading itself and what it takes to become a more successful trader. I will explain about the history and key terms of the industry, point out the Do's and Don'ts as well as discuss different trading approaches and help you to decide which might be the most suitable for you. Finally I will introduce you to an interesting trading strategy which I call "Hopscotch", because it bears many similarities with the infamous children's game.

At the beginning however we take a look at the industry to determine what factors influence your success as a trader. I will compare seemingly unrelated items such as gambling to give you a new perspective on the profession you are about to chose.

I will try to give you a comprehensive understanding about the facts concerning this domain. I will clean up some of the misunderstandings and misrepresentations that have been propagated over the past few years. Finally I will provide to you the necessary basics on your way to becoming more successful.

The first six chapters will give you an overview of the industry and the characteristics of trading itself.

Chapter VII through X discuss what it takes to become a trader and what kinds of trading styles there are as well as several successful strategies that I have come across in the last five years.

Chapter XI will elaborate on the Hopscotch strategy that gave the book and radically new software for traders its name.

The Appendix provides you with an entry into the industry lingo and some basic knowledge about technical stock analysis.

I have had my share of success and failure in this industry. Anyone who claims that he has never lost any money is probably omitting some information. It is because of my failures that I am successful now. It is my hope that you can lessen the impact of the mistakes you will make simply by reminding yourself about what you are about to read.

Here are some interesting facts to start with:

According to a recent study there were 40,000 Day Traders at the end of 2001, 20% less than two years ago. They account for 1/3 of all NASDAQ and NYSE volume. About 83% of this volume is done by 4000 individuals who can be categorized as semi professionals who are mostly ex-wall street people. They trade either proprietary funds of a day trading firm or their own capital and execute 25 to 50 trades (buy & sell) per day. 66% of these traders work with/for proprietary money. With roughly 2.5 to 3 billion shares traded Day Traders move approximately a whopping 1 billion shares everyday!

Upwards of 90% of all individuals who ever engaged into direct access-trading lost all or most their money within the first six months. This is even more remarkable since this was already true during a time when the market seemed to go nowhere but up. How could so many people loose during a Bull market? And to whom?

The market participants who are continuously the most successful in this domain now for the better part of ten years are the institutional investors and proprietary trading floors/ hedge funds which trade intraday as their every day profession. In comparison the numbers of continuously successful individuals are negligible. Why is that? And what differentiates the successful players from the rest of the pack?

The majority of the individual traders are now pursuing their goals from their home office. Five years ago they used to gather on trading floors. Why did the return home? And does it have any impact on their performance?

The euphoria or as Fed-Chairman Allan Greenspan once said irrational exuberance is long gone. The bubble has burst. Day trading has altered its appearance and is staging a comeback, this time better prepared and more concerned about its clients. Who are the predominant players today? And what are the most significant changes in the industry?

The world-wide-web provides an ever growing audience with financial advice, decision support, "insider"-news and proprietary chat-rooms and message boards. Many of the providers claim to have the only recipe to become a successful day-trader and they are compensated well for their services. Is there such thing; the Holy Grail; as an ultimate formula for successful intra day trading? And if so, why haven't the public media reported about it?

After spending many years in this industry I think it is time to try out something new. I analyzed all the methods I had learned about and combined the seemingly best of many strategies to make a new one, Hopscotch. Which leads me to the following question, would children really make the better Day Traders? And if so, what would their approach be?

I will try to provide answers to all of those questions in the following chapters.

Chapter I

How could so many people loose during a Bull market?

As everyone recalls, until the year 2000 the US experienced the longest economical expansion in its history. The stock markets kept rising accordingly. At the hype of the Bull market the NASDAQ Composite Index gained an incredible 80%+ within a 1-year period. The Dow Jones Industrial Average Index also gained significantly over the years; however it did not loose all of its gains like the NASDAQ Composite Index.

Everything seemed so simple. You buy a stock, hold it and then sell it for a profit. In a rising market this task should be very attainable. In short, that is how you do it, but it is not what happened.

Almost ten years ago a new industry; day-trading for individual investors; made its debut in the securities industry. At first it was a rather cumbersome process. Interested individuals opened up and funded a trading account. They then gathered in the offices and branches of their respective brokerage. On these "trading floors" they basically called out buy and sell transactions to a terminal operator who would communicate and confirm these trades with NASDAQ. Software and computer hardware was not sophisticated enough yet to offer these traders a comprehensive overview on the market at any given moment. These hurdles prevented the average person form participating. The majority of traders at that time were ex-professionals with a shrewd understanding of the market and substantial background education in the financial industry. This initial group of a few hundred people was basically as successful as their professional counterparts in the big New York brokerage firms. The big players humored these rogue traders as outsiders and did not consider them to be any threat towards their own profitability.

Then everything changed. The day trading brokerages started offering proprietary software that would allow their customers to participate in real-time in front of their own trading station on the brokers trading floor instead of shouting out trades to an operator. The ever growing processing capacity of pc hardware and wider availability of connectivity allowed individual traders to use software that gave them the impression of equality to New York professionals who had been sitting in front of those screens for many years already. All of a sudden the brokers could basically take as many new individual accounts as they could fit seats onto their trading floors. Whereas before they were limited to the number of people a single operator could handle. This started the beginning of the end.

New brokerages applied for licenses, branch offices popped up like mushrooms all over the country. The number of ex-professionals however was limited, so the industry targeted a new kind of client to fill up the seats. "Do you have $ 50,000? Would you like to make thousands of Dollars a month by simply sitting in front of a computer screen?" Advertisements in the print media and news reports on TV propagated how anyone; from the untrained housewife with an inheritance to the retired executive with a recently unlocked retirement account, yes anyone, could make money sitting in an office and "simply" trade a couple of stocks every day.

This caused a landslide. More and more people joined the flock. And it changed the composition of the group substantially. Before we had a small group of "rogue" professionals, now the majority of these traders we comprised of individuals who did not know the next best thing about real-time stock trading or the technology involved to support the action. Three things happened:

1. The brokers made bigger profits, since more clients generated more tickets.
2. The electronic exchanges experienced a never seen increase in volume with NASDAQ soon overtaking the NYSE.
3. Individual traders started to loose huge amounts of money.

In fact a vicious circle began in which the losses kept growing up to a point where these people lost everything.

Obviously the brokers and the electronic exchanges did not complain. But if so many people lost money; why did they loose? How come no one found out about it for several years? And why did these people not simply stop trading before it was too late?

There are several explanations. Any profession, plumbing, accounting or brokerage is subject to the same equation. When starting out as a new business 75%+ of these first time entrepreneurs fail in the first twelve months and have to fold their business. These numbers apply to professionals, now imagine what happens if hundreds of untrained people attempt to pursue a new business. Just by these standards most individuals were doomed to loose most or all of their funds in the attempt to become rich as a day trader.

The reasons why individuals would do even worse than professionals are also simple. Money has a very special place in the hearts and minds of people all over the western hemisphere; in fact so special that we seem to hold it above all other things in life. Whenever an item takes such a special place, our decision taking process is usually beyond reason. When we start to take financial decisions with our hearts instead of our brain, disaster strikes.

Imagine you purchase a stock, and the stock price rises, as a day trader, you should of course decide when to exit in order to actually realize the profits you see on your trading screen. However your psyche tells you that you might loose out on any further increase, so you keep holding on. Before you know it, this intra day trade mutates into an overnight position. As long as the stock keeps rising you continue to postpone your sell decision and prevent yourself from banking any profit. Often times the little profit you could have taken the other day has turned into a loss because overnight the stock turned against you and is now below your original entry price. Human psychology struck again... Now you keep telling yourself that you can not sell the stock since you would realize a loss. After all it will come back...and come to think of it, it was already that much higher, so yet again you keep holding on instead of covering your losses quickly. Before you know it the stock falls further. Now you ask yourself why this must happen to you, why your stock and not one of the 10,000 others which at this moment all seem to look much more promising than the one you hold. You keep agonizing yourself a little longer but finally when it is almost unbearable, you bail and instead of making a little money, now you lost big.

The fact that your broker allows you to trade with leverage, offering you a stock trading line of credit, in some instances of up to ten times of your actual account balance, adds to your distress. If you have a $ 50,000 account balance and purchase stock for $ 200,000 and you end up losing 10% on this position, you in fact lost 40% of your money. During the hype of the Internet bubble stocks like Yahoo, Amazon, Ebay, Priceline and others experienced moves of 10 or more % within a day regularly. Since everyone wanted to be involved with the "hot stocks", a few bad trades as described above and your account was empty before you even had a chance to learn from your mistakes.

The professionals on Wall Street operate free from these concerns. First of all they do not trade their own money. For them it is just a job, the money is just a number on the screen. They have an emotional distance. Their employer gives them a firm set of rules on how to execute trades. All they have to do is follow these rules. Then they will keep their job and get paid.

THIS IS VERY IMPORTANT!!! If you ever want to become successful you have to set yourself in the same state of mind as a professional.

Why did no one find out about all these people who lost money? There was a huge cover up!!! Not like you might think. The brokerages did not have to do a whole lot with it. The individual traders themselves are the culprits. In the US people admire success or at least the facade of the same. People who lost money lied to their spouses and friends and even drove themselves into self denial. They simply kept re-funding their brokerage account every time the money was gone. They took individual loans, maxed out credit cards and signed second or third mortgages. On the face of it they pretended that everything was going well. Remember they were under peer pressure, and all the other guys did the same...

At home losing was a non-issue. If a loving husband would confide to his wife about losing their savings, she would probably break a fight and argue that she told him that this would happen all along. After a few minutes of shouting the fight would be over and the wife would have retreated into her chambers, if not to "her mother". "If you lose money day-trading there will be no warm food and no sex at home" That was a bon mot some of my fellow traders used to recite every now and then.

Funny enough it never occurred to anyone to question the statements of all these successful people. Mathematically trading on the stock exchange is a zero balance equation. For every Dollar that someone has made during a single day someone else must have lost exactly that Dollar. With everyone claiming to be a winner, there had to be something wrong.

But why with all these odds against them and with individual cash reserves dwindling fast did these people continue their hopeless journey? Besides the peer pressure that may have strangely forced people to continue pouring money into this ditch, day trading has a lot of similarities to gambling. Addiction, people were addicted to trading they had to come back to the office for yet another day, no matter what the cost....

If you compare compulsive gambling the similarities are striking. Provided you recognize your new job of being a day trader as a profession, then you would say you earned your money in case you experience success, or not? However when people talk about making or loosing money they use the words winning and losing, typical gambling terms. Traders ask each other frequently about which stocks they would "play" or have "played" today. Instead of handling real money the trader "handles" digits on a screen, just like he would gamble with plastic chips instead of Dollar bills. The terminology alone makes it strikingly clear. Many individuals recognized trading as a game instead of taking it as serious as the profession it really is.

And then there is this adrenalin rush. Once you put your money on the line, you can feel it igniting your body. Just like during the moment you place your chips before the croupier starts to push the roulette dial. I talked to a rather successful trader in Austin. He was a professional and had made substantial amounts of money in his time. I asked him why he would still get up early in the morning and take the stress of trading hundreds of positions each day. Obviously he did not come for the money anymore. He answered:" I need the rush! I have not missed a single day of trading in the last three years, even when I travel I stay connected. I can not do without the excitement, not a single day."

Combine addiction and self denial and you have a recipe for tragedies.

When the Internet bubble finally burst, everything came to the light with a vengeance. People attempted to sue their brokers. Armed clients who had lost their money, home and family to their addiction gunned down employees and former fellow traders before ending their own lives. Congressional inquiries were launched and changed the perception of this once so glorious industry dramatically.

Back to our original question where did all this money go? Of course, "the money is not gone, it just belongs to someone else..." that was what my senior colleagues told me at the bank where I worked as an apprentice, and this statement holds true in this case as well. If all these individuals lost money and the Wall Street houses kept reporting profits, then obviously the money went to the institutional investors. Opening direct access trading to individuals in order to eliminate any unfair advantages brokers may have had before the change of the securities act had exactly the opposite effect. Not only did the brokers profit the most from this changed legislation, everything happened even faster, because of the leverage and the self feeding frenzy which grew account and participant numbers exponentially. It seems that the United States has a long history of making things worst whenever the legislators want to liberate the consumer. Energy, Communication and Securities-Trading all these industries were liberated only to experience some kind of disaster shortly thereafter. Once the disaster occurs fingers are pointed and then, finally appropriate measures are put in place to gradually improve the situation back to normal.

Day trading is good business. You can be successful as a day trader. You just have to be aware of the pitfalls that come with this territory.

Be aware of your opponents.
Educate yourself to the highest degree possible before engaging in any life action.
Treat it like a job.
Trade without emotion.
Set firm guideline both for the profit and loss you are willing to take.
<u>And more important: Execute according to those guidelines.</u>

Chapter II

Why are the professionals more successful?

Daa...They are professionals. Just like we expect top athletes in Basketball or Football to outperform weekend players we should not be surprised to find that Wall Street professionals are at the top of the pile when it comes to extracting profits from the stock market.

Professionals enjoy many advantages over individual day traders. First of all they receive a proper education before they are allowed anywhere near a trading post. For starters there are the SEC licenses every professional trader is required to pass. The reading material to acquire these licenses already provides a good basic understanding of the industry terminology and the meaning of these terms. In addition many of the new professionals have attended industry related post grad education in business and or management studies. Now all of the above are things that you as an individual are able to obtain yourself. The course material for the SEC tests is widely available. In case you did not enjoy any business studies, you can purchase specific books about economy, market or stock analysis. With some hard work you are able to level the playing field up to this point, but from here on out the individual day trader leads an up-hill battle against his Wall Street opponents.

The technology used on professional floors seems to be only little different from the Level II trading applications individuals use today. However the differences are quite significant. First of all there is the connectivity. Individual traders today work mostly from their home offices through DSL or sometimes only Dial-Up Internet access. Wall Street brokers have multi redundant direct lines with seemingly unlimited bandwidth to the stock exchanges. The software is also quite different. While Level II trading platforms provide quite a deep insight into the market, Wall Street professionals have substantially enhanced systems at their disposal. While individual traders are only able to see the first tier of any offer or bid of a Market Maker on NASDAQ, his Wall Street counterpart will see exactly how his peers have positioned their available shares or bids throughout the various price levels of a stock. Needless to say, that this extra knowledge can give you a lot of re-assurance. If you would know that an important Market Maker like Goldman Sachs for example is just short of offering another 900,000 shares in a specific stock you might reconsider your decision to trade or avoid this stock. Without this privileged knowledge you could simply find yourself fighting a losing battle in which you try to match your 1,000 share position against the millions of shares that might stand against you.

This single example clarifies why the little guy has only an outside chance when trying to defend himself against professional traders. And it teaches yet another lesson. If you can not win fighting against them, fighting with them is a better course of action.

If you don't want to be overrun by the big guys, your best chance for survival and maybe even success is to run with them. In fact try to stay in their wake. Just like driving behind a truck, your car experiences less wind resistance and completes the journey with less fuel consumption. You only have to be aware of the next move of your new "big friends". If they suddenly break or turn, you need to make sure you get out of the way in order to avoid being run over yet again. In trading terms this means two things. First of all you need to observe the market carefully once you are in a position and adhere to the exit strategy that you have laid out for yourself before you even entered the trade. Second you need to set your guidelines realistically and stay only invested in the market as briefly as necessary to achieve your realistic goal. The key word is realistic. No professional trader expects to make several Dollar of price increase in a stock within a day, and neither should you.

In fact, professionals spread their risk. They can afford to do so much easier because they have rather deep pockets, you don't. So the only way to spread your risk about many positions is to have all these positions consecutively rather than all at once. This means, stay in trades only for short amounts of time and trade multiple times during the day. With this strategy you are able to follow in the wake of your "big friends" many times every day. Provided that you have sound guidelines to execute your trading decisions, you are now much closer to the professional players on Wall Street.

The markets have crashed and the terrorist attacks of September 11, 2001 have dealt a second devastating blow to the markets. Only now, in early 2003, the markets begin to recover some ground. Strange enough, while we would have expected brokerage firms to make profits in climbing markets with all the facts we have established until now, how come that they also incurred trading profits during the last two years where the NASDAQ almost lost 70% and the S&P 500 also fell approximately 40%? Again the answer is quite simple.

As we all know you can make profits in a down-market by short selling stock. However, individual traders avoid trading short positions. While mathematically a short and a long trading position are not much different except for the order in which the buy and sell transactions are executed, psychological concerns hinder the individual trader from capitalizing on these opportunities. It is against human nature to sell something that you don't already have. After all, what if it turns out you can not buy it back later? Well again, if your strategy dictates what to do in case of a certain profit or loss, you should always be able to close a position, no matter whether it is long or short. The abstinence from short trading hampered the ticket revenues of brokerages but had no influence on profits off trading their own funds. If you analyze the markets carefully you will find that prices fall actually faster than they rise, which in turn means that the opportunities to capitalize on a falling stock can be swift and more profitable than on a climbing one. Professionals only care whether there is action in the market that allows them to execute trades one way or the other. As long as the markets are active and show a decisive direction on any given day, professionals will engage into the action and continue to harvest profits for their firms. Individual traders on the other hand will favor climbing markets and avoid trading activity during other times. This is a bad habit. Considering that trading is your profession it would be a lot easier to make a living if you were able to participate every day and not just when the markets rise.

As pointed out in the previous chapter a professional trader acts free from emotion. Rather than executing trades based on a wild hunch or because a friend recommended it, brokerages have worked out firm strategies and guidelines on how to find and execute trading opportunities. While these strategies may vary among the brokerages, the simple fact that they at least have a strategy, and more important execute it, sets them apart from the majority of individual traders. We will discuss potentially successful strategies later on, however the first milestone is to have a strategy and adhere to it at all times. Having a strategy is the easy part. I believe every trader has some idea about what he would like to do and how he would like to do it, but the moment he gets into a trading position his brain stops and all the psychological skeletons leave the closet and take control from here on out. After yet another defeat the individual regains composure and probably kicks himself for not having stuck with the original plan for the day.

This chapter reinforces some of the previous rules and adds some more:

Trade without emotion.
Don't fight the big players, trade with them and not against them.
Look for active markets.
Learn to trade long and short positions alike.
Develop a strategy
And most important: Execute your strategy.

Chapter III

Why did the individual traders return to their home offices and how are they doing?

As explained in Chapter I, trading floors for individual traders mushroomed and people flocked into these novelty offices. With the decline of the markets and the burst of the Internet bubble many traders have lost all their money and returned to their old jobs. But there is still a lot of money out there that continues to seek new ways of increasing profitability. Yet the seats in the offices remain empty in fact many offices have closed since the ultimate hype in the industry is gone. While the brokerages still hold about 30,000 accounts which are eligible to participate in direct access trading only few people still come into the remaining trading offices on a regular basis. With the improvements in technology and the availablity of cheap and fast computer hardware individual traders are now able to put together the same technical setup they enjoyed only on trading floors before. Many brokerages now charge seat fees and it is actually cheaper for individual traders to stay home and experience about $ 1,500 as a one time expense for a pc and pay maybe $ 60 a month for a DSL. More important, people save the time to commute and they can direct their attention to other things during market hours with less trading activity. Since many brokerages offer their trading software free of charge provided you hold a minimum account balance or execute a certain number of trades per month, staying home is the new way of life for individual day traders.

Never the less trading all by yourself is dull. We are social animals and require daily attention. In lack of the personal contact traders experienced on the trading floors they have reverted to joining chat rooms and message boards, sometimes with some buddies for free on other occasion they pay hefty fees of up to $ 500 per month to have a seemingly experienced leader who tells them what to do.

Today individual traders in the US mostly rely on their trading software for real-time quotes. They focus on stock newsletters and TV for additional information.

The trading software technology has reached a plateau after several years of development. The act of executing trades has changed only little over the past two years. The media have dramatically changed their reporting over the years. With the introduction of full disclosure many of the "insider" news people were counting on in past years has now become available to professionals and individuals alike. The general consensus is that if everyone receives the news at the same moment, then there is no need or better yet no opportunity to take advantage of the situation.

Television is still a big part of day trading. The predominant station for individual and professional traders to watch is CNBC. The station has captured the attention of millions of viewers. People keep their TV on to follow the various shows during the whole market session every day. CNBC's coverage of the ever climbing NASDAQ towards the end of the last millennium further fueled interest and participation of the day trading community. Journalists like Mark Haines, Joe Kernen, David Faber, Ron Insana, Maria Bartiromo, Bill Griffeth, Ted David, Tom Costello, Robert Pisani and many more gained cult status. Sometimes a comment they made, no matter how unimportant, actually started to affect specific stocks. One must point out however that the journalists do not make the news, they just deliver it. And it is also important to note that the CNBC team prides itself in researching stories before airing them. It seemed that at first the journalists themselves did not realize the impact of their work. Mark Haines stated in a recent interview for CBS that when CNBC started broadcasting over a decade ago, their only audience consisted of Wall Street professionals. Over the years growing public interest added viewers from all ages and professions. At the height of the Internet bubble everyone from housewife to CEO was glued to the screen. While CNBC still maintained the highest level of professional journalism Haines admitted that in the late 1990s it really did not matter what analysts or invited CEOs would have to say about a company. The mere fact that a specific stock received some airtime caused its stock price to soar. I guess this shows that it takes two to make a successful couple. CNBC certainly did its share, but many viewers failed to actually listen to the messages. To better appreciate the professional pride journalists take in their work the public must understand that financial journalists can not engage into any short-term trading activity, preventing them from taking any personal advantage of news that they may learn before others.

Channels like CNBC are very helpful to individual investors. CNBC provides a comprehensive overview of the markets. It is one of the easiest ways to find out about the general market mood. Regardless which stock you trade. If you want to follow the professional traders in their activity the best way to learn about that is from listening to what the journalists have to contribute about the general market situation.

The importance of chat groups has significantly increased over the past two years. There have never been more commercial offers to join a chat room or news group than today. These groups are not free from concerns however. It has been a known fact that some chat room conductors actually influenced their followers in a way which allowed the conductor to capitalize in addition to the chat room fees. How? Very simple, first the conductor would buy a low volume trading, little known stock. Then he would announce this stock as a great buying opportunity and while his followers send out buy orders and push the price higher the conductor already closes his position for a nice profit. After that he declares this stock to be no longer interesting and his followers start selling. Some of his followers also make money, but most do not. Performed on a massive scale a conductor can become very wealthy. Today good chat rooms make the trading activity of their conductor transparent and provide a trading record to prove that the conductor does not front-run his own customers. Despite this minimum of decency that you have to expect from any chat room you join, it is very hard to determine what makes a good chat room. There are many strategies and as long as they are well executed many of them provide the opportunity to extract profits from the stock market. The most important thing the chat room really provides is the peer pressure to act professional. As an individual you fall victim to your psyche all too easy and are very likely to abandon your strategy. But with the certain knowledge that other individual traders and even the chat conductor had the professionalism to close a losing trade or to take a profit out of the market you are more likely to take your profits as well or admit to your losses before they put you out of business.

The trend towards trading from home has not greatly affected the numbers of individual. It has however affected the way they make trading decisions. I believe that today the traders are less likely to jump onto any band wagon simply because someone else says so. The speed with which newcomers lose money in the market has definitely declined.

We learn that it does not really matter where you are located as long as you have a decent technical setup. And yet again this chapter reinforces the fact that successful day traders rely on a strong strategy which they adhere to under all circumstances.

Chapter IV

Why did the bubble burst?

At first glance this question does not seem to have anything to do with what this book is all about – day trading. However, much blame has been put on the traders for running the market up and down between 1996 and 2003. The following pages illustrate the various other culprits one might want to take a closer look at before putting all the blame on the traders.

As with many topics these days it is never just a single reason or event that could be declared to be responsible for the burst of the stock market bubble and a market decline that took the NASDAQ composite, the former poster child of the world's markets, from its rocket ride beyond 5000 back down close to 1000 points a mere three years later. I will try to give you a few different perspectives to the issue and let you be the judge what really caused the bubble to burst and bring North America the worst stock market performance since the great depression in the 1920s and 30s.

For those who believe in technical analysis of equities the explanation is really quite simple. Throughout the second half of the 1990s the stock market value increased at an ever steeper rate year over year matching a parabolic graph on the chart. The Elliott Wave Theory (please refer to the Appendix) clearly states that market movements occur in wave patterns. And those wave patterns occur in cycles. In other words - What goes up must come down. Shortly before and after the burst in early 2000 technical analysts would appear on CNBC and talk about NASDAQ going to 1000 points. They were mocked by many. Three years into the market decline the laughter has stopped.

Another simple reason is of course that the true value of any merchandise is eventually discovered. With the expansion of the Internet virtual business was the future of the economy. No matter how ridiculous a business idea was, if it had a dotcom at the end people were willing to through money at it. In 2000 it became clear however that most of these businesses are nothing but hot air. Of the thousands of internet ideas only very few have survived and even fewer still have a value that is worth mentioning. Ebay, "the first global flee-market" is probably one of the few corporations that have truly proven the validity of its concept. But the other 99.9% have not. They were never profitable and probably never would have been. Shareholders and investors grew tired of waiting for the end of the rainbow. Many resented pumping money into companies that would use it to show their employees a good time with recreational zones at work and corporate benefits others don't even get when they take a room in a Spa resort. So the money stopped coming and these companies closed their doors.

Fraud and conspiracy are also often mentioned as the stumbling block of the legendary 80% increase in market value in 1999. But how? Everyone knows the securities industry is one of the most regulated and scrutinized industry in the United States. The various schemes that became apparent over the past two years are proof for two things: Laws are there to be broken. And there is always room for a loophole. I believe everyone has followed the rise and fall of Enron. They actually used the oldest scheme there is – cooking the books. With thousands of subsidiaries, tax shelters and special purpose entities the balance sheet of Enron became a maze in which auditors and government officials alike got lost. But crime does not pay. Eventually the scheme was discovered and Enron went from billions to bust.

This brought another widely recognized effect with it, the domino principle. Enron was the first domino in the row. Now with everyone becoming suspicious people started to poke into the financials of publicly traded companies and set off the chain of dominos and soon other companies followed suit. In the new millennium we saw the largest corporate bankruptcies in history. Luckily the indiscretions of some corporate executives were only grave enough to harm the company's stock price, but at least these companies are still around and all is not lost. Tyco, Martha Stewart Omnimedia and Imclone come to mind.

Another now well documented scheme was the rigging of IPOs. In the late 90s everyone was desperate to get in on the action. But there were only so many shares to go around for an IPO. In addition the firms entrusted with placing the IPO wanted to ensure that it will be a success, which in return would bring new companies to the table and with it taking those public for a hefty commission. These two facts made a terrible combination. The underwriters would offer certain clients preferred treatment when it came to allocation of IPO shares without any lock-up period. In return these clients had to promise to buy deeper into the stock if it hit a pre-determined price within a specified time period. Of course right after fulfilling this commitment the clients were free to dump all of their shares at any time. Let's say Newco was scheduled to be underwritten at 10$ and of course the book was over signed by 20 to 1 for example. The underwriter already knew, that Newco's opening price would be probably closer to 40$ once free trading starts. So he offers his larger clients a deal. "You get a larger portion of shares for the pre-opening price of 10$ each, but in return you have to promise to purchase X thousand shares once the stock crossed 20, then 30, then 40, then 50$. After that you are free to sell all of your shares at any time." Of course for these clients it was a fire-sure winner. While they might have taken a slight hit on the last thousand shares they bought over 50$, they obviously made a humungous profit on the initial partition of IPO shares. So they agreed and with each agreement they ensured that they will be cut in when the next IPO comes along. The average investor who was not this lucky had to get in on the open market for what we now know was oftentimes an artificially inflated, rigged price. Eventually of course somebody blew the whistle. And since the market is on its steady way down, IPOs are few and far between anyways.

Another possible factor is the blind belief in bad advice; in this case investment advice. The same brokerages who made money underwriting the IPOs also issued valuations and recommendation. A favorable recommendation would raise interest in the stock and increase its price. This would make the CEO extremely happy and when it came to seek the advice for the next corporate transaction the brokerage whose financial analyst made the call had better chances of making money with the corporation it recommended to the individual investors. The scheme worked. But it also only went so far. The brokerage industry recently worked out a settlement with the government with financial penalties of epic proportions. The financial industry was only too glad to pay up and settle. A federal law suit and sentence would have opened the doors for millions of investors to pursue class action law suits in the trillions of Dollars.

Finally there are the economy and geo-politics. With Bill Clinton presiding over the longest economic expansion in American history people felt that there was no end to it. The US was the powerhouse of the world. Economies in Asia and Europe were failing left and right. Yet America produced a budget surplus and the nation was on its way out of debt. In short things could not be better.

And then something went wrong... Whatever your personal political orientation may be, I believe it is fair to say that the vote-counting scandal of the presidential election between Mr. Bush and Mr. Gore was awkward to say the least. When it turned into a court battle at the end of which ultimately the Presidency of the United States was assigned by court appointment, not only many Americans but also the rest of the world was uncertain how to interpret what happened. You know that things must look ridiculous if of all countries Fidel Castro's Cuba, a long time enemy of the United States, offers to send observers to help with the democratic election in the United States of America. Don't get me wrong. I am not making a statement on whether the wrong or the right man got the job. I am just saying the way how the job finally was filled was wrong. Any self-respecting democracy would probably have discarded the tainted election process and repeated the election, which on several occasions the United States itself has requested emerging democracies to do in similar situations.

After Mr. Bush had taken office the geo-political cards just did not seem to be favorable to the United States. Armed with a new political doctrine which pillars were American military superiority at all costs and the right to strike at a time of his choosing in order to prevent any and all threats, economical, political or military, aimed at the United States and its citizens Mr. Bush set out into the world. While most people of other nations like the American as an individual, many now feel deep resentment towards the United States as a country. And with an ever growing number of countries and people offended by the policies of Mr. Bush's government, heads started to steam. This pressure was released in what is now a fix-point in history; 9/11. In addition to the loss of life and grief it caused, this event at the beginning of the new millennium destroyed more than one trillion Dollars in stock market value and caused the demise of whole industries. Again I want to make clear. I strongly resent any kind of terrorism as a means to achieve political objectives. And there can be no reason, religious or otherwise do ever justify what happened. With the benefit of hindsight even high-ranking government officials have to admit that the signs were there and that a different foreign policy in combination with better intelligence may have prevented this terrible event. 9/11 was the pretense for war, first in Afghanistan and then in Iraq.

Terrorism, its prevention and wars have at least two common denominators, they cause uncertainty and cost a lot of money. Domestic and global demand declines, consumers abstain from consuming, investors lose faith in the stock market. This makes for a downward spiral of the economy and its stock markets.

I believe more probable explanations for the stock market decline can be found. Personally I think that a perfectly timed combination of all of the above caused the markets to decline in the way they did.

Where do we go from here? After the rain comes the sunshine. If this was a book about long-term investment, I would recommend starting the build-up of stock positions. With prices so low one should start to get back in. Not with all of his money of course, only 1/3. Should the market go down even further, you have enough left to average down. Should the market go higher you have at least a foot in the door and did not miss out on the next bull market.

For intra-day trading purposes it is not really important whether we go up or down. As long as you are able to determine where the market is going in the next few minutes or hours, you will always be able to make a profit.

Chapter V

The industry today

The early day of the day trading industry was like the Wild Wild West. Even though there were laws and regulations, people had little experience in applying them to a vast number of individuals. Anyone with $ 50,000 and later even as little as $ 10,000 who claimed to know how to push a button on a keyboard was allowed to join in and risk his money. Since there seemed to be an unlimited supply of fresh blood the brokerages cared little about the high drop-out or better blow-up rate among their customers. But as the fresh supply dwindled and the regulators threatened to come after the brokerages new guidelines were established. Today brokerages expect the individual traders to prove a minimum knowledge in written tests or to provide trading records that prove a certain number of years in hands-on day trading experience before being allowed to open a new direct access trading account. Of course the original regulations about being a qualified investor with either a certain net asset value or income are taken much more serious these days. Many brokers have joined forces with trading schools where new account holders have to attend and pass a virtual or personal class. These classes are very sophisticated these days.

Chart Analysis, Trading Patterns, Background on Technology, simulated trading sessions and much more is being offered for free. Three or four years ago all of this cost $ 1,000 and sometimes in excess of $ 5,000 per class. These are definite improvements everyone should welcome.

There have been more changes, and they are for the most part behind the scenes. In the beginning the day trading brokerages were considered a sideshow act by the big Market Makers and Retail broker firms like Schwab for example. Casually dressed guys with important titles led these new and sometimes very small firms. Everything was quite informal. It was not uncommon for a new customer to have the CEO or at least a high executive of the firm on the phone when calling in the first time. Then with branch offices mushrooming and numbers of traders exceeding 10,000 some of the brokerages turned out to have a better customer approach than others. Before long the market was roughly divided among about 100 brokerage firms of which a mere 5 held more than 80% of the customers.

At this time interest for day trading reached its peak. CNBC had daily segments devoted entirely to day trading. The word was almost magical. Everyone knew what a day trader was. Everyone wanted to be a day trader. The mere fact that you are a day trader guaranteed you the respect of bystanders. It was at this time that something phenomenal took place. Charles Schwab Inc. one of the most renowned and largest retail brokerage firms of the US announced that it had purchased a Texas based brokerage and trading software firm. Besides the fact that the employees probably celebrated for several days because their stock options turned them into millionaires the implication of this buy-out were much bigger. This was as if knighthood had been awarded to this industry. For the first time the big Wall Street firms acknowledged that this market is important and can add a lot to the bottom line of any major brokerage house.

This also meant that play time was over now. With serious players taking over the arena the image of the day trader had to change. The day trader a rogue mercenary who lives by his own rules and was supported by equally independent thinking brokerages was no longer acceptable. Furthermore, in April 2000 the stock market had just collapsed. And everyone blamed the day traders who supposedly manipulated markets and drove the stocks so crazy that now every hard working American had to pay the ultimate price. The hero had now turned villain, the word Day Trader was no longer fashionable in the media.

A new word had to be created, Direct-Access Trading. There it was the original word which seemed not hip enough to generate the initial demand and had been hidden in the basement was now resurrected. It sounded more professional and sincere. If you visit the websites of day trading brokerages today, you will hardly ever find the word day trading on their web pages. Everyone is a Direct Access Trader now. Even the media has made the transition. Only in isolated case the old word is used to help some new viewers understand what the journalists really mean. A friend of mine always says "If it walks like a duck and quacks like a duck, it is a duck, no matter what you call it" But the changes behind the scenes guarantee better conditions for all individuals. The improvements in providing trading education are the single most important step the brokerages have taken towards their customers.

Today there are significantly less brokerages than two years ago. Minimum requirements have to be met, but they are not all alike. In general it is recommended to go with one of the bigger ones since the standards are higher.

Chapter VI

Is there a Holy Grail of day trading?

Yes and no. What? Please come again....

As pointed out before there are many successful professionals in the stock markets. And just looking at the number of traders, stocks and trades which interact with each other every day it seems very unlikely that there is this one formula or the one strategy that leads from rags to riches. Obviously there must be more than one!

In Chapters VIII through X we will take a closer look at the differences between some of them. For our immediate purposes it is much more interesting to find out whether all these different, yet successful, strategies have something in common.

Indeed they do. As pointed out many times before the key to a good strategy is that you actually use it. It is a little like playing the lottery. Chances of winning may be very slim, but then again if you never play the lottery you can not expect to win either. So if you have a strategy, by any means you must use it and follow it to the very point. The moment you do, you will know exactly that the rate of your success can only be related to the guidelines within your strategy. By changing the guidelines little by little in a trial and error effort you should be able to optimize any strategy.

Why are those strategies not widely publicized?

We previously established that the most consistent performers are the professionals on Wall Street. As you can imagine, Wall Street does not have the least bit of interest in explaining to the public how exactly they extract profits from short-term trading. So lets see if we can lift the curtain and get a glimpse of what is going on behind the scenes.

What are the key components to any strategy?

Be aware of your competitors

In other words you need to observe what the market as a whole is doing. If everyone is selling out on a specific stock it would be quite foolish of you to believe that you can turn things around. If you plan to purchase 1,000 MSFT shares and all of a sudden every Market Maker and many other individuals start selling the stock then you need to acknowledge the situation and act according to your guidelines. With several millions shares on the sell side it might be a foolish move to buy the stock just this moment. The price could simply drop well below your threshold before long. There is no point in entering into a trade that is doomed before you begin. You as an individual can never beat the market. If you can not fight against the market (Market Makers), then you need to fight with the market.

Go with the trend. Find those areas of the market where it is easy to tell the story. If the overall market is going up, find stocks that are outperforming the market, this must obviously be where the action is. In a downtrend find stocks that under perform even below the market and yet again you should be right in the center of the action.

Very important; look for familiar names of big companies. Professional traders rarely trade small stocks or low volume items, they just like you don't want to be stuck in a position simply because there is no market for it. Trading the biggest 100 or 200 maybe even 500 stocks on a volume basis is where you should find the big Market Makers showing their activities. That is where you want to be.

Every now and then you will find a "hot issue" a stock that trades way above its usual daily volume. Even though this may seem like the place to be, act with caution. Check out whether there is big news out or whether it is an IPO stock with trading restrictions. The big Market Makers usually do not support these stocks with a lot of volume. The volume in those stocks is mostly generated by your fellow traders. Stay away. Successful strategies all lie with the big Market Makers. If they don't trade theses tocks, neither should you.

Risk Diversification

You have heard this probably many times, but just to refresh your memory, "Don't put all your eggs in one basket." The professional traders manage enormous amounts of money. They spread these funds into many positions at any given time. This minimizes their risk substantially. Should they miss an important trading signal or should a specific industry sector or stock have unexpected and influential news then at best only a small fragment of their account is at risk. It is obvious that with the limited account sizes individual traders have that they can not spread out over 100 positions for example. That however is not necessary. Try to work with three or four positions at any given time if your account is not big enough to handle more. Make sure that you execute many trades and don't get stuck in a specific stock. That way you could still trade 20 or 30 positions over the course of a day and spread your risk quite well by comparison. In any event you should never try to take on more positions at any one moment than you can comfortably handle. People grow with the tasks they accomplish if your account and abilities allow you to start with only two or three positions at a time, then your growing experience and hopefully your growing account balance will enable you to step up to four, eight or more simultaneous positions over time.

Elimination of greed and fear

Greed to try and make more and more profit on a single trade. A professional trader has a preset exit strategy. This exit could be marked by a certain profit or the occurrence of a specific incident during trading.

Example: You buy a stock at $ 50 per share and the moment you profit equals $ 1 per share you get out.

For the moment the stock price stops rising in your favor and drops more than $ 0.10 below its recent high you get out.

Fear from losing everything. A preset strategy prevents you fear from gaining the upper hand.

Example: You buy a stock at $ 50 per share and the moment you loose more than $ 0.25 per share you get out.

Now remember these are just examples. The actual profit/loss you can afford to take greatly depends on the size of your account. The smaller your account is the tighter you have to manage your risk.

In any event we are talking about day trading, so what happens if none of your preset exit points is reached during the trading session? Well, then just get out before the market closes, there is no use in holding an overnight position. First of all it will tie up your available buying power for the next day but most important you can not possibly forecast what will happen tomorrow. The most tragic example is what happened on September 11, 2001. That morning trading never even began and was suspended for a week. When the market finally reopened many stocks had dropped anywhere between 10 and 30%. Now as a day trader you would not have felt any financial impact. Since the markets never opened your cash balance would have remained unchanged. Anyone who held a position that morning however went through some serious pain and had to stay with his positions for almost six month before coming back to pre 9/11 levels. That meant no profits for six months.

Chapter VII

Is day trading something I can do?

If you are not ready to take the risk of day trading then this is not for you!

Realize that when you enter the market you are at risk of losing all of your investment capital and money that you borrow to trade. It is important to know that during the learning curve it is almost a given that you will incur losses, if you cannot afford the risk of those losses than day trading is not for you.

If day trading creates permanent unease it is not for you!

Knowledge about the market and the ability to use the keyboard accounts for less than half of what it takes to make money in the stock market. This is a stressful career, one that can eat you from the inside. You will know quickly if day trading is for you or not. A successful day trader can take a step back and make decisions without using emotions or opinions. You must be logical and without emotion. If this creates permanent unease for you, then trading is not for you!

If you typically have a high stress level or often worry then day trading is not for you.

If your personality is one where you are typically high strung you must be forewarned that day trading is a very stressful job. If you have difficulty handling high levels of stress you might want to think of a different career.

If you are gambling, this is not for you.

The day trader must be able to stick to the strategy they have made for the market, be able to think logically, and must take all emotion away from the trade.

Chapter VIII

What kinds of trading styles are there?

There are 4 different types of day traders:

Discretionary Traders:

This kind of trader uses intuition to make trades. Advice from others is also used in the decision making process. For example: A friend might say that they think a stock is going to go up and the trader uses that information to make the trade. At first some do profit from using this method but almost always they end up losing in the end.

Technical Traders:

These traders use more technical data to make their decisions. Integrating charts, indicators, the news, and decision support software to make trading decisions. Often times traders will use back testing to compare how indicators have done in the past. The trader might even develop some rules but is inconsistent in following through with them.

Systems Traders:

As with anything there are rules to increasing the chances of becoming successful. The Systems Trader has learned to make and strictly follow a specific set of trading rules. These rules are based on methods that have been proven

to work in the past. This trader manages risks
and understands that there is no "Holy Grail"
for trading. Part of trading is losing; it is in
managing those losses that he becomes
successful.

Fundamental Trader:
Fundamental traders are hardly found in the
direct access trading community. If you trade
based on fundamentals you try to determine
whether the book value of a certain company
matches with its stock price. However even
though this determinations sounds easy it
usually takes a lot of time to do the legwork
and with today's rules of accounting it has
become more difficult to distinguish between
reality and pro forma numbers. Also it usually
takes substantial amounts of time until the
market recognizes that stocks are over- or
undervalued, sometimes months or years. As a
Fundamentalist you would simply sit out those
periods, which obviously defeats being a day
trader.

Chapter IX

Different Trading Strategies

Scalping or Grinding

Most common trading strategies when day trading began and the spread between Bid and Ask was still large. Short-term trade, that can take a few seconds. Trading time is usually under 5 minutes. The trader profits on short-term momentum and movement of stock. You must be in & out quickly!

Advantages:
> Fast
> Your money is out there for less time
> You can use your money more often during the day

Disadvantages:
> Small Profits
> Must go at larger share sizes to make a profit
> Larger share sizes increases your risk. For many traders they have to use a large chunk of their investment money all on one stock if it goes down you can lose big!

Breakout Trading

When using this strategy the trader finds stock with a chart pattern that looks like it is going to breakout to the upside or breakdown to the downside. In order to detect a trading opportunity a trader needs to look for stocks that test support and resistance lines.

Advantages:
>   If done correctly this strategy could potentially make more money than scalping.

Disadvantages:
>   You must have a technical ability to analyze charts
>   You need experience
>   Timing is key you have to know when the stock is beginning and ending a trend

Don't be greedy know when to get in and out!

The Golden Cross

This trading strategy usually works the best for short-term trades. In order to recognize a trading opportunity, a short-term chart of the stock is needed. To allow this analysis, two Moving Averages (MA) need to be added to the chart. If it is a 3 minute chart usually 8 and 16 or 15 and 30 ticks for the Moving Averages will provide the information needed. The number of ticks will depend on your specific chart settings and the data feed provider. In the example below two charts are displayed. They are 3 min bar charts with a fast Moving Average of 8 ticks (red line) and a slow Moving Average of 15 ticks (green line).

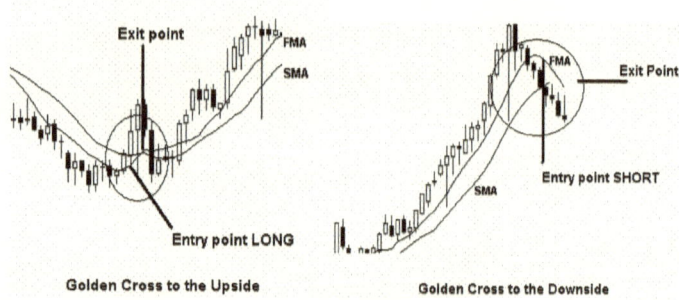

Golden Cross to the Upside   Golden Cross to the Downside

Whenever the fast Moving Average (FMA) moves too far away from the slow Moving Average (SMA) and then turns around to approach the slow moving average in an angle of approximately 90 degrees, the stock is likely to either move up (left chart) or down (right chart) significantly. As soon as the fast Moving Average starts to turn (entry point) entering into the position should offer the opportunity to participate in about ½ to ¾ of the move the stock makes. The safest exit point when the trade is already profitable is usually when the two Moving Averages cross each other or short after that (exit point). Staying in too long could result in failure. For example notice in the left chart, right after the cross the stock drops back down.

Advantages

Once the chart box is set up correctly, this trading strategy is very easy to apply.

Disadvantages

Often times a trader will miss his exit point and end up flat or even down in his position. Trading Golden Crosses needs a lot of discipline.

Trading on News

Using current events and news to aide in your trading decisions. Upon good news the trader goes LONG. Bad news should cause a trader to SHORT the stock.

Advantages:
It is easy to listen to the news and follow. An excellent supplement to the other tools you are using.

Disadvantages:
The news isn't good enough, stocks will not always react in the way that the media thinks.

Position Trading

Mid-term to long-term trades. Most commonly based on charting, chart patterns, or fundamental analysis. Don't confuse position trading with investment trading. Investments usually last over very long periods of time (months or years) if you do those you are not a day trader.

Advantages:

You do not have to be a fast trader since you trade to make a profit off several dollars per share it is not as crucial to get in or out quickly as it is for scalping.

Disadvantages:

Your money could be tied up in this position for one or more days leaving you no room for short-term trades. If you are wrong you could incur substantial losses. It takes a lot of experience to do position trading well.

Since many of these styles require knowledge about charting the Appendix will include a comprehensive summary about technical analysis.

Be warned: Different strategies employ different triggers. Sometimes the conclusions reached in one strategy may stand in total opposition to what another strategy advises you to do.

I encourage you to continue reading all the chapters of this book before you decide how to proceed.

Chapter IX has given you a glimpse of what traders will be taught on their way to becoming Wall Street professionals. And the Technical Analysis section in the Appendix makes this journey even more daunting. However there is a way out. All you really need are the following two chapters. They provide you with everything you require to find your way into this industry. Why then make you read all the other stuff? Well our society is about having choices. I promised to provide you with a comprehensive overview of this industry and its teachings. After reading the whole book you should be able to make an educated decision on whether this is really the profession you want to be in and if so how you will become more successful in it.

Chapter X

Summary of the most important rules regardless of the trading strategy you plan to apply.

The Market Is Always Right
Don't try to go against the trend, stay with the market. If the trend is down go SHORT. If the trend is up go LONG.

Always Go LONG On Strong Stocks
Select stocks that are increasing. If it looks like it is building momentum, go LONG. If the stock is down don't go LONG because you "think" it has to go back to a previous price. If a stock is down or weak go SHORT instead of LONG.

Always Go SHORT On Weak Stocks
Select stocks that are decreasing. If it looks like the momentum is weak go SHORT. If the stock is up or strong go LONG instead of SHORT.

Never Chase A Stock Price To Get In

When you have determined at what price level you want to enter into a position but your order is not executed because your stock has already started to move in the direction you had predicted. Do not chase the stock in order to buy it at any price. It is very likely that you will end up in a position that you do not want anymore, for a price you don't like, once your hunting instincts have been satisfied.

Analyze All Of Your Trades

Try to explain to yourself what you liked and did not like about your actions concerning each trade. Look for obvious errors like keyboard mistakes as well as the errors you will find on this do and don't list. Only by recognizing your mistakes you will be able to learn and not repeat them.

Don't Get Greedy

Take your wins and go, do not shoot for the moon or get the quick win. If you have made money there is nothing wrong with getting out. You can always get back in.

Be Patient

Do not get into a trade just to trade. You do not have to be trading all of the time. Have a reason and a plan as to why you are entering. Do not get in just to play. As Edwin Lefevre said "There is the plain fool who does the wrong thing at all times anywhere, but there is the Wall Street fool who thinks he must trade all the time"

Be Aware Of The Time Of Day

Always know what time it is and when you need to close. Don't enter into a trade if there isn't enough time to get out.

Always Approach The Market With A Plan And Then Stick To That Plan!

Discipline, Discipline, Discipline

If you make a plan, stick to it!

Keep Your Losers Tight

If you are losing get out. Put limits on the amount of loss you will take and follow it. If the stock goes against you, the reasons that made you go in are no longer valid GET OUT!

Losers Always Have To Be Smaller Than Your Winning Expectations

If 90% of your trades are profitable and 10% are losers but the losers are worth more than your profitable trades than you have failed overall. If you keep the losers smaller than the winners you will succeed overall.

No Emotion

Don't become emotional about the stocks you trade.

Take As Many Trades As You Can

The only way to participate in the market is to be in the market – this does not mean that you have to trade just for the sake of trading itself. If there is no reason or prospect don't just trade.

Trade Both <u>LONG</u> And <u>SHORT</u>

Trade Stocks That Have High Volume

If you stay with high volume stocks you will always have someone to trade with. If you are in a profitable position you cannot realize that profit until you are able to find a buyer to close the deal.

Think About Why You Are Doing This Job

Set A Reasonable Goal For The Month

Break your goal down to each trading day. Whenever you have reached your goal stop trading for the day and "Go Home". You can practice in demo mode for the rest of the day. As you feel more comfortable increase your goal still stick with it. Your goal should match your skill and your account size. Do not set a goal that is unreasonable. Only increase the goal if you are continually making the goal day after day!

Chapter XI

The Hopscotch Strategy

After utilizing most of the strategies mentioned in this book, I noticed that most of them require either a specific talent or that the strategies can only be applied successfully during very specific market conditions. This was a problem. I needed a strategy that would be easy to apply every day and offer plenty of trading opportunities at the same time. After all, this is my profession and I need to have at least a realistic chance of bringing home the bacon. You will find that the Hopscotch strategy incorporates various aspects of other more complex strategies while maintaining simplicity and avoiding contradictions that usually occur between the different strategies. I want to point out however that I can not claim the genius of inventing the basic outlines for this strategy. I merely tweaked some of the rules so they would be more applicable to the average individual trader. The praise for actual strategy belongs to the professional traders and institutions who have utilized similar techniques successfully for many years now, only on a much larger scale.

A friend of mine said "Well this Hopscotch of yours is great it does seem to work, but trading like this is actually pretty boring." He is correct, but given the choice what would you rather be: exciting & losing or boring & profitable?

Hopscotch is really a simple game. Children play it with great success all the time. According to the game rules the objective is to jump and place your foot safely within the marked borders of the 8 to 12 chalk squares while avoiding the square that has been marked as a no landing spot. Sounds real easy! – And it is.

If you transfer these rules into the stock market they would read like this. Put your money into the right sectors of the market at the right time. Sounds easy, doesn't it? But how is it done? Before we answer that question I want to point out that the following strategy is generic in its nature. While the following pages use the stock market as an example, the generic rules of this strategy will apply to any financial market and not just to stocks.

Let's dissect the rules and look at all the aspects of this game.

Just like the chalk squares, the stock market has sectors, e.g. Banks, Oil, Retail, Internet, Communications, etc. And each sector then includes a certain number of stocks. With the rules and strategies explained in previous chapters you now know that it is much safer to trade stocks in baskets instead of putting all your eggs in one basket. The general idea is simple. If you look at the market at any given day, certain sectors will stick out. If in an overall positive market the Retailers are mentioned as being particularly strong, then obviously the retail stocks must outperform the market on that day. Buying a mix of retail stock therefore seems like the prudent trading decision. Why? If the market continues to go higher, then it is likely that a strong sector will continue to outperform the market which in turn will give your trades a greater success potential. Should the market fall back, a strong sector is less likely to fall at the same pace. This allows you to get out and cover your position with no or less damage than on a merely average trade. Of course a similar strategy also works for a falling stock market. In that case you identify those sectors that are falling even faster than the average market and short a mix of stocks in this/those sector/s. Your protection is also similar. Should the market drop further, then it is even more likely that a sector traders "hated" to begin with will fall even faster. Should the market climb back up, then this well "hated" sector will rise slower and you will be able to cover your positions with no or little harm.

The jumping in the Hopscotch game is synonymous with a fast moving pace. You have to place your money on the right market sectors and find the most efficient ratio between the time your money is in the market and the profit potential. Why?

1. It is much easier to predict or anticipate the move a sector or stock for the next maybe 20 minutes instead of trying the same for a timeframe of lets say two days. Take the weather for example. If you had no additional information other then looking out the window, it would be far easier to predict what the weather will be like 10 minutes from now compared to what it would be two days later. The same logic applies in the stock market. Since you do not have the magic eye, your anticipations are also only based on the current information you have, current index and sector values, stock prices and charts.

2. Whenever you place your funds into situations that you know not enough about, you increase the risk. In Day Trading the risk increases obviously with the time you spend in a specific position. If it does not move, you are not making money and of course you tied up your funds preventing yourself from finding profits in other trades. If it moves against you and you don't act in the belief that the move is only temporary you may be stuck for a long time. When holding overnight positions the risk is even greater. No one knows how political or

economical events overnight will affect the positions you hold. By the time you find out it may just be too late. Take Roulette for example. Statistically it has been proven that there is no system to win in Roulette. The odds are stacked in favor of the house. Not to bet money would be the safest way. But if you must bet, then your best chance would be to bet only one time, on color for example. With 37 numbers, 18 red, 18 black and one green your chances of doubling your money are approximately 48.64/51.36 for one bet. If you would continue to play, then you would multiply this disadvantage of 1.36 against you. It is a game of chance, but with the odds against you it will be only a matter of time until all your money is gone. So keep your exposure short and crisp.

Ok, now that we have the general picture, we will work on the exact recipe on how to identify trading opportunities and capitalize on the same. This following section will be easier to execute for novice traders than for semi-educated or experienced folks. Novice Traders simply do not carry any baggage (previous knowledge) around that might confuse things.

Let's start with the basics.

You will require a trade execution software, preferable with charting capability (if not, then a separate charting software will do).

You should have a trading account with sufficient funds to allow you holding at least three stock positions at once.
While practicing this strategy you should definitely lower your shares size. E.g. if you usually trade 1000 share positions then cut the size in half. Novices should not exceed 300 shares per position to start with. Having said that, with stock prices being in the cellar many brand names currently quote in single digit Dollar amounts. Since with such prices percentage moves will only make a stock price move by the penny, you may choose an alternate strategy for determining the share size. In this case you would for example set a fixed Dollar amount for a position rather than a specific share size. In any event, this limit should be set in such a way that you are again able to hold a minimum of three to four approximately equally large positions with your buying power. Obviously you will have to pay brokerage fees. With such small position it is likely that your gains will not actually cover the costs. The point of practice is to get the hang of it. If you are making a profit before commission on these trades, then simply increasing the share size will make these trades profitable after commission once you get into

the groove. Practicing like this is and gaining experience a lot cheaper than trying to be a player and blowing your account before you even had the chance of comprehending your new profession.

Even though this strategy should be applicable to any sector or stock it is always safer to concentrate on those stocks that trade on good volume. It is important that you are able to get in and out of your positions without any problems. If there is no one you can sell your stock to, it will be hard to realize your profits or cover your losses in time. The less experience you have, the higher this benchmark should be. An experienced trader will find it easy to execute a trade in stocks that trade as low as 100,000 shares per day, whereas a novice would be better off staying with stocks that have a daily volume above 4 or even 5 million shares. This narrows down the scope of the task ahead of you considerably. NYSE and NASDAQ list almost 10,000 stocks however maybe only several hundred fulfill the volume criteria. There is one important exception you must observe. Stocks that are in the news typically have unusually high trading volume. The trading direction of these stocks may coincide with the markets, however trading on news is a very unpredictable business and it is therefore safer to stay clear of these "hot stocks". This is not to be confused with General news on markets or sectors that do not specifically target a single company.

If you follow the markets closely you will find that the most active trading occurs during the opening and the close of the stock exchanges. Those are the times that you want to trade as well. After all if there is no action in between it should be a lot harder to find trading opportunities during the off-times. Typically the first and last 90 to 120 minutes of the market hours are best suited for trading the Hopscotch strategy.

With these basic parameters in place we will now direct our attention to actually identifying viable opportunities. Once the markets have opened we will look at the main indices, Dow Jones Industrial Average (DJIA), NASDAQ Composite (NASDAQ) and Standard & Poor's 500 (SP500). The direction of these three indices should give us a fairly good understanding of the direction the general market is headed. Most of the times, all three indices will actually point into the same direction. If not, then the direction of the SP500 and the NASDAQ are more important, because the DJIA only includes 30 companies versus a combined 1000+ companies in the other two indices. With the direction of the market established we now look for sectors that outperform the markets. On an up day we look for sectors that are even stronger than the market overall and on down days we look for sectors that perform even worse than the market. An old proverb on Wall Street says "The trend is your friend…". As with most proverbs, there is some truth to this one as well. So make sure you look into the right direction. As mentioned before there are many sectors in the market. Here is a list of the more important ones in no specific order.

Finance, Biotech, Retail, Drug, Forest, Boxes, Internet, Semis, Transport, Oil, Telecom, Technology, Utilities

Each of these sectors is represented by a sector index, which means that you should be able to find a ticker symbol for it. This will allow you to pull up information about sectors on your charting software. Since there is a multitude of data feeds out there, I am unfortunately not able to provide you with the appropriate ticker symbol for each sector in the various data feeds. On CNBC you will also receive sector information in the Sector Watch segment which is regularly presented over the turn of the day.

Once you have identified a sector as being particularly strong on an up day or particularly weak on a down day, you then turn your attention to the stocks within that sector. Of course not all of them, only those that fulfill the volume criteria set in the beginning. And again you will identify those stocks that are by comparison outperforming the sector they are in.

The easiest way to actually make these comparisons is to look at charts. The charts should overlay the index/sector or sector/stock you want to compare. Per definition a stock that outperforms another stock or sector shows relative strength. A stock that underperforms compared to another stock or sector shows relative weakness. In the following I have depicted all the possible scenarios you will encounter when comparing indices, sectors and stocks. It is recommended to use an Index with a broad base such as the S&P500 for these chart comparisons. I have also included a recommendation for the course of action for each scenario.

Uptrend – Stock and Index move identical

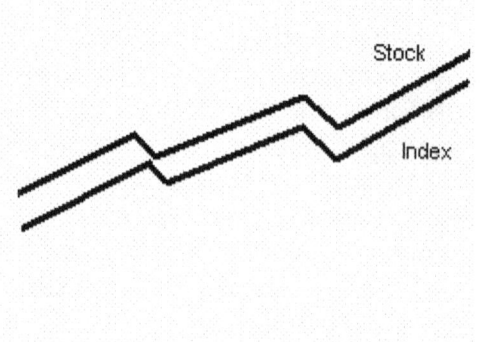

In this scenario the stock has no relative strength or weakness. Its moves are almost identical with the Index. Since we can not predict the next move of the Index a decision to take a trade is difficult.

Uptrend – Stock shows relative weakness

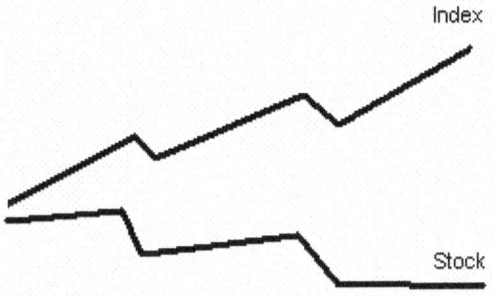

In this scenario the stock does not move to the upside as much as the Index. The stock's moves to the downside are bigger then the pullbacks of the Index. The stock shows relative weakness. A short position may be profitable but it takes additional information before deciding on such a trade. Finding a stock with relative strength in an overall uptrend may involve less risk. However, when taking a short position, mind your stop-loss carefully!

Uptrend – Stock shows relative strength

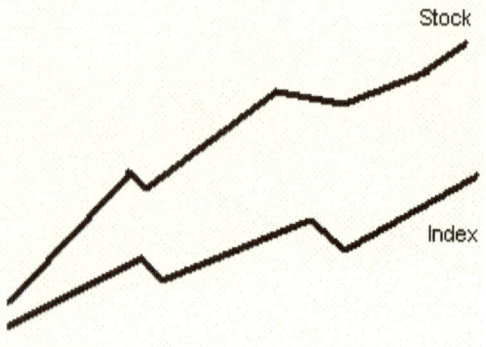

In this scenario the stock moves stronger to the upside than the Index while losing less when the Index pulls back. The stock shows relative strength on an uptrend day. Should the Index fail, it is likely that the stock will not move lower at the same pace or might not even move lower at all. If the Index advances once again, it is likely that the stock will make another strong move to the upside. Taking a long position once the next pullback occurs may be profitable. Mind your stop-loss in case the Index and/or stock fail!

Downtrend – Stock and Index move identical

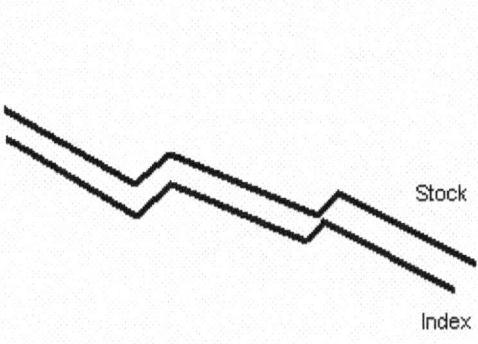

Stock

Index

In this scenario the stock has no relative strength or weakness. Its moves are almost identical with the Index. Since we can not predict the next move of the Index a decision to take this trade is difficult.

Downtrend – Stock shows relative strength

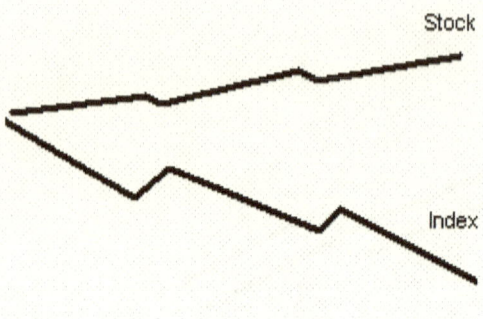

In this scenario the stock does not move to the downside as much as the Index. The stock's moves to the upside are bigger then the bounces of the Index. The stock shows relative strength. Taking a long position may be profitable but it takes additional information before deciding on such a trade. Finding a stock with relative weakness in an overall downtrend may involve less risk. However, when taking a long position, mind your stop-loss carefully!

Downtrend – Stock shows relative weakness

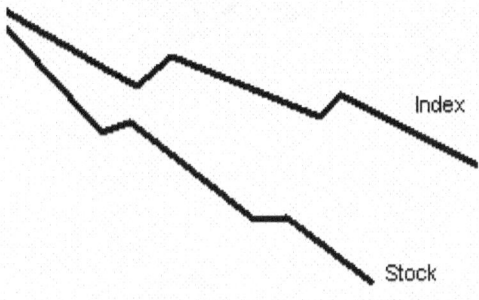

In this scenario the stock moves stronger to the downside than the Index while gaining less when the Index bounces. The stock shows relative weakness on a downtrend day. Should the Index have a major bounce, it is likely that the stock will not move higher at the same pace or might not even move higher at all. If the Index fails once again, it is likely that the stock will make another strong move to the downside. Taking a short position once the next bounce occurs may be profitable. Mind your stop-loss in case the Index and/or stock bounce!

Trendless

Neither the stock nor the Index show a decisive trend for the day. In a trend less situation it is difficult to predict the next move of any stock or index. A decision to take a trade is difficult.

With these seven simple scenarios we are now actually in a position to make trading decisions. In fact we should now be able to get into a position. Now all we have to do is get back out of that position and possibly make a profit on it....

The setup of your trading screen will have some impact on your ability to comprehend the data you see and determine your execution. Many traders swear they need a multitude of windows on their screen. I have seen traders using up to four screens at the same time with as many as 30 or even 40 open windows, all displaying streaming data. I have to admit I used to be one of those guys too, using two screens with about 20+ windows. As always too much of a good thing, in this case information, can actually be bad for you. You may simply miss out on many opportunities because you can not process all this data. Your computer may become clogged and actually display the information delayed. Even if this would only be ten seconds or so, it may have a significant impact on your ability to get in and out of trades. Finally the conclusions you draw from various windows may contradict each other and ultimately leave you paralyzed when it comes to making your decision.

The Hopscotch strategy is about simplicity and focusing on the core data. You will need no more than 4 to 6 windows from now on. This strategy requires a Level II Box, a Chart Window that allows overlay comparison, an Execution Box to get in and out of trades, a Trade Blotter to monitor your open positions, maybe a High/Low List to check on the red or green colors flying by for market direction AND finally if you do not wish to screen the stock market for trading opportunities by yourself the "Hopscotch Box". In addition you listen or watch CNBC for example to make sure you don't miss any news that might push the market into sudden and unexpected directions. This simple setup should give you a comprehensive platform to start with. The arrangement of the windows may also be important. A lot of traders like to cruise over their screens either clockwise or counter clock wise instead of making zigzag moves with their eyes. Here is an example on how the screen can be setup. You start at the top left with the High/Low List and/or Hopscotch Box. Now you compare the trading opportunities in a Chart Box on the top right of your screen. Provided it is a valid opportunity you enter the ticker symbol in the Level II Box on the bottom right of your screen and determine at which point to actually get into the trade using the Execution Box which is either integrated into the Level II Box or located right next to it. If successful your new position should pop up in the trade blotter on the bottom left of your screen. To make things easier, many trade blotters allow you to set custom alerts to notify you about certain issues with your open positions. By using such feature you are free to concentrate on finding trading opportunities while your trading platform assists you to determine when to close your positions.

Just like we observed a strict set of rules to get into the trades we need an equally firm definition to exit a position, **regardless whether we make a profit or loss**. This is actually more difficult than getting into a position. Once you hold a certain stock, you are always in danger of getting emotionally involved and the human psyche will try to persuade you to do the wrong thing. When you find yourself losing your psyche tells you to see it through because the stock will come back. When you are making money your psyche will dictate to stay in because there might be more money to be made. You would be ill-advised in both cases. **Set yourself a stop loss!** Depending on your financial capability this stop loss may vary. Another factor to determine the stop loss is also the actual profit expectation you have on your average trade. Since we are talking about intra day trades that last anywhere from one to thirty minutes on average, your profit expectation should be anywhere between $ 0.15 and $ 1 per share. In order for things to work not, your stop loss must obviously be lower than your profit expectations. Lets assume for a moment this strategy would be no good or you would be unable to identify the right stocks every time. Then according to statistical probability your random choice should cause 50% of your trades should work in your favor and 50% would work against you. With a stop loss that is smaller than your profit expectation you should at least manage to maintain your account while getting better at what you do or refining your strategy. Of course with a good strategy you should be able to improve this 50/50 ratio in your favor. At that point you would definitely be banking a profit at the end of most days. A good rule to have low risk exposure is to keep your stop loss at or below 1% of your trading account balance (NOT buying power!). Why? Even with ten open positions going against you, you will never harm your account beyond the point of recovery. Besides banking profit your goal must always be to live and be able to fight another day. For most traders this stop loss is probably between $ 0.10 and $ 0.50.

So if you get into a trade and this trade turns against you, don't think twice and exit this trade when your stop loss has been reached. Use your money to find a better trading opportunity.

When you look at a profitable trade similar rules apply. Even though the chart depictions were simplified you will find that markets, indices and stocks typically move in waves. E.g. if you hold a long position and the prices go higher, the stock will retrace at a certain point. Just like someone who tried to run fast might pause and take a deep breath before running further. There is no need for you to stick around and wait to find out whether your stock is just taking a breather or is really pulling back to eat up all your profit. Simply observe your profit margin and the moment the stock pulls back from the most recent highest level of profit by more then 10 to 50ct (at the most) get out of that trade and bank your profit. If that same stock appears on your radar screen again later you can always get back in. Unrealized profit is no profit at all. You can only spend the money which you have taken off the table.

So at all times observe your open P&L (Profit& Loss) in the position manager of your trading software. Once your exit points are hit, execute without looking back.

One more thing, many people think that the experience with the keyboard for trade execution is very important. With a strategy like this it is not. First of all you only find yourself in stocks that are usually well guarded by large institutions. There should be no sudden unexpected moves that could capsize your account. Second, over the years the trading software has become very smart. With the push of a button some trading platforms will find you the best possible price at any given moment totally automatic. Some platforms even allow you to set exit parameters. "Trailing Flags" will be particularly helpful for this strategy. This would allow you to basically "fire & forget" once you have opened a position.

Before concluding this chapter let me summarize the General Rules for the Hopscotch strategy.

1. The stock you intend to trade should trade on good volume.
2. The sector index of the stock you intend to trade and the majority of the other stocks in that sector MUST trade in the same direction.
3. Don't trade "Pump & Dump" stocks. (Stocks with specific big news.)
4. Always trade stock basket and not just single positions.
5. The best moment to enter into a trade is when the stock takes the next "breather". Don't get in too fast.
6. Should a trade not work out: **TAKE YOUR LOSS QUICKLY**
7. Exit a profitable trade once your stock shows signs of "stalling" into the direction you trade. Remember once the stock resumes course you can always get back in.
8. Banking profits is an important part of a good strategy.
9. Don't repeat mistakes. If you have selected a market direction you trade and it does not work out for several trades in a row, then re-examine the situation before trading into the same direction again.

Why is this such a great strategy? It is based on easy to follow rules and has clear and identifiable entry and exit points. It works in strong and weak markets. This is probably the most important reason. A strategy should work in as many market situations as possible. As a professional trader you have to make a living with your business. If you don't have a strategy that allows you to trade almost every day then it might be difficult to generate a consistent income. There are really only three scenarios during which even this strategy can not help you.

1. On trend-less days. If there is no action, you can not expect to make money with any strategy.
2. On "Greenspan Day", whenever the Chairman of the Federal Reserve Bank is scheduled for a major interest rate decision and/or hearings on Capitol Hill you should try to stay out of the market at least until after his comments are broadcasted.
3. During extreme market conditions (market gaps up or down with futures limit down or DJIA curbs in effect to the upside at the open) trading into the obvious market direction is less likely to succeed. Should you trade into the given market direction in these conditions with several trades in a row not working out in your favour, then re-examine your strategy for that day.

Sometimes it may be best to take no action or try trading into the opposite direction in these situations.

An experienced trader should be able to generate consistent profits with this strategy. I found that typically about 65 to 70% of my trades are profitable with Hopscotch.

A novice trader might have less upside in the beginning. But for him more important is to survive the learning process and protect his trading capital until he fully comprehends his new profession. Like in any new business, one can not expect to generate large profits right away. Most new businesses experience a negative earnings situation in the beginning, why should the trading business be any different. As mentioned before 90% of all new traders lost most or even all of their money. On the other side, of those traders who survived the first six months more than 50% were still in the industry after 12 months. By using a simple strategy like this you may just increase the odds for your success to 50/50 from an otherwise unfavorable 90/10 against you. Once a trader has reached that level, his results should show steady improvement.

A "childish" approach sometimes does make a compelling argument for becoming a more successful trader......

When I started using this strategy, software was less advanced I actually had to do all the steps described above manually. It takes some time and sometimes you will miss out on a trading opportunity because you are still analyzing the situation, but it can be done. However with the advances in technology I have been able to feed all these rules and equations into a software application. The software scans the markets and only reports those sectors and stocks that actually look like potential trading opportunities. You in turn only have to look at this final selection, which should not take more than a few seconds, compared to maybe 10 or 15 minutes of screening the market manually over and over again. In addition the software includes a chat that lets you compare your trading decisions to those of other traders, which should ultimately improve your trading even more. During the beta testing phase with traders in North America and Europe it became clear that everyone was looking for more automation. We therefore included a fire & forget functionality that allows each trader to send out his own customized basket trades with preset trailing stops to safeguard each position after it has been established. Compatibility with more trade execution platforms is continuously improved. The software is called HOPSCOTCH, what else.

It is readily available at www.hopscotch.cc to find out how you can take advantage of this comprehensive tool.

Final Thoughts

I think it has become very clear especially over the last few chapters of this book, that direct access trading can either be very tricky, elaborate and sophisticated or just as simple as playing Hopscotch in the driveway of your house. Well over 100 pages have gone into this book, however if you memorize the seven Hopscotch scenarios as well as the nine basic rules a napkin would have been sufficient to give you a new perspective...

Sometimes it is necessary for us to take the long way home to realize that there are easier alternatives.

And... Yes, children would be better traders!

Appendix

1. Technical Analysis

Charting

The attempt to forecast the future direction of a particular index or stock by recognizing chart patterns. There are various charting techniques to support the trader's decision process.

- **Support and Resistance Lines**

- **Channels**

- **Triangles**

- **Elliot Wave Patterns**

- **McClellan Oscillator**

Support and Resistance Lines

Commonly used by brokers and individual traders. Recognizing these possible turning points for a stock could be of great help to prevent you from losing money. Since most of the brokers apply this technique automatically, the movement of a particular stock often times becomes a self fulfilling prophecy that you DO NOT want to go against. Here is an example for a support and resistance line in a chart pattern. Typically, you would try to find a price level where the stock either bounced off (Support Line) or withdrew from (Resistance Line) in the past and then simply draw a horizontal line into your chart. When the stock approaches any of these lines again you now know that it is running into support or resistance.

This chart depicts Support Lines:

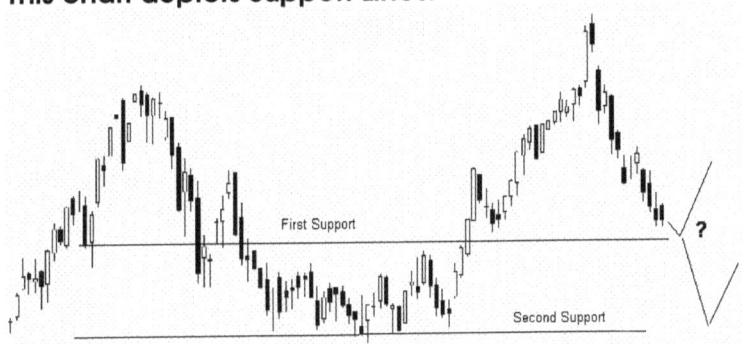

First Support

Second Support

?

The stock is about to test First Support. If it bounces off it is a good LONG opportunity. If it fails it is a good SHORT opportunity and the exit point would be at Second Support. Second Support is much stronger because the chart bounced off that support line several times in the past.

This chart depicts Resistance Lines:

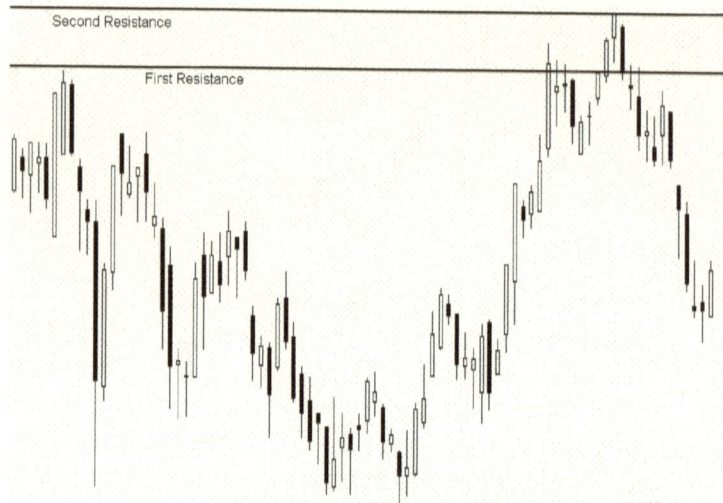

Second Resistance

First Resistance

The stock tested first resistance and failed with a drawback right to the bottom of this picture where it ran into support. The second attempt to break First Resistance resulted in several tests and a minor drawback before the stock finally broke through. If a stock fails to break through resistance it becomes a good SHORT opportunity. If it breaks through First Resistance it can be a LONG opportunity. Sell when it reaches Second Resistance.

Fibonacci Lines

Leonardo Fibonacci was a mathematician who lived in the middle ages around 1200 BC. He discovered several formulas that are being used even in today's modern world. His most important discovery was the sequence of integer numbers (each number is equal to the sum of the preceding two: 0,1,1,2,3,5,8,13,21,34,55,89,144...) Deriving from this sequence he discovered a ratio today known as the Golden Section or Divine Section. The ratio is 0.618. Based upon this ratio calculation, the Fibonacci Lines are applied to the charts. Since a lot of professionals apply this particular technique, stocks tend to exactly fulfill "the prophecy" of these Fibonacci Lines once applied.

This Chart depicts Fibonacci Lines

To draw a Fibonacci Line you have to enable
the Fibonacci feature on your charting
software (if available). Connect the two most
recent extremes (As shown above 1 & 2). Your
software will then apply the lines accordingly.
The lines you see will help you to detect LONG
and SHORT opportunities just like regular
Support and Resistance Lines.

Channels

As long as a chart moves within a channel the channel lines most likely become the turning points for the chart movement. Whenever a chart hits Line A and bounces off it is a LONG opportunity. Whenever a chart hits Line B and fails to break through it is a SHORT opportunity. Once entered into a trade you know approximately where the stock is about to turn again enabling you to have an exact target of your exit point.

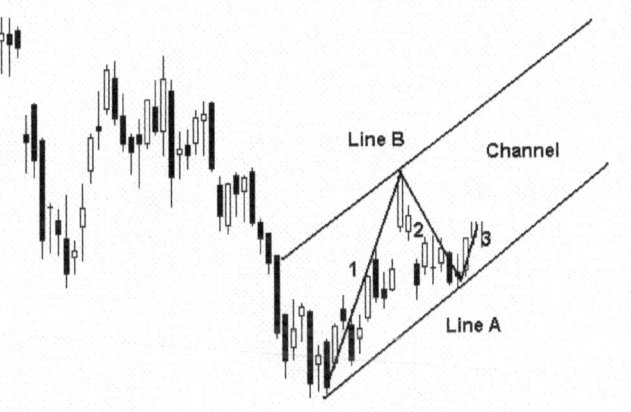

Draw a line from the beginning of Wave 1 to the beginning of Wave 3 (Line A). Draw a parallel line through the beginning of Wave 2 (Line B).

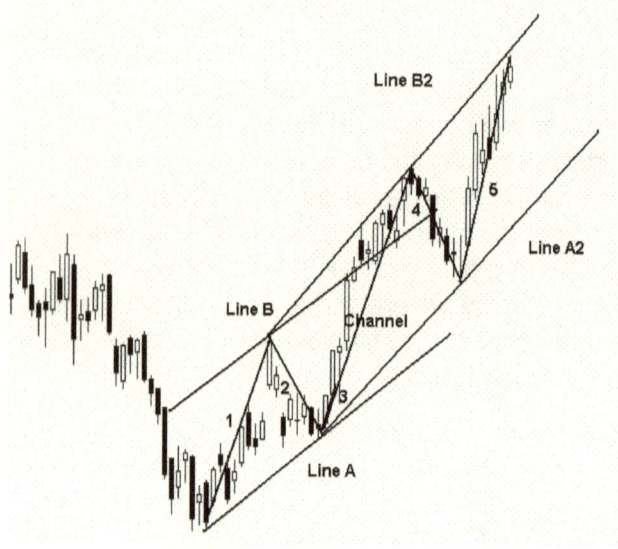

The above picture displays the same chart at a later time. Once the 3rd Wave breaks through the first channel the channel lines have to be adjusted. To do this, draw a line from the beginning of Wave 2 to the beginning of Wave 4 (Line B2) and a parallel line from the beginning of Wave 3 (Line A2).

Triangles

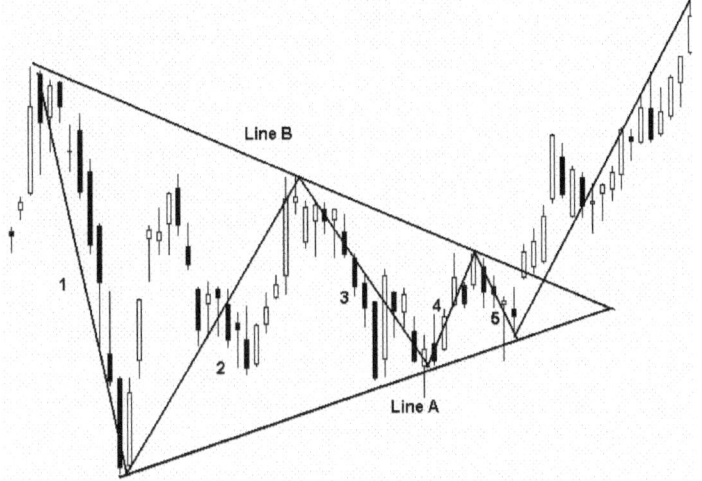

Usually, a triangle pattern cannot be recognized before the turn at the end of Wave 3. At that point it becomes clear that applying knowledge about channeling would result in a triangle because the waves are contracting. Once the chart reaches the end of the triangle a LONG opportunity arises. This can be seen in the chart above, notice how the chart breaks above Line B. If the chart breaks Line A than it results in a SHORT opportunity.

Elliot Waves

The Elliot Wave system of empirically derived rules for interpreting action in the stock market

The charts run in a pattern of five impulsive waves into the general market sentiment and a correction of three corrective waves against the sentiment. This technique is the most effective when applied to indices in order to recognize the general market trend. Applied to a specific stock chart the system is still working but a lot of deviations from standard patterns make it more difficult to forecast. More experience and market knowledge is necessary to succeed with this technique when applied to a particular stock chart. Impulsive waves (waves going with the trend) are counted 1,2,3,4,5. Corrective waves (waves going against the trend) are counted A,B,C.

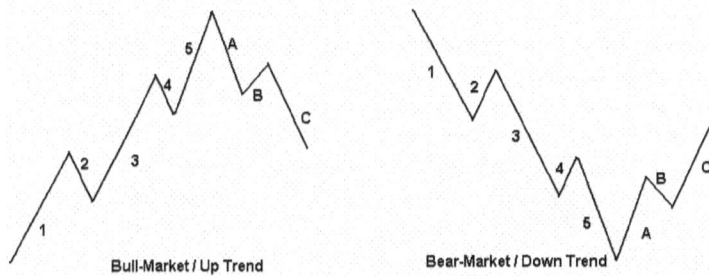

Bull-Market / Up Trend   Bear-Market / Down Trend

If the market trend is up you will see wave patterns of five up and three down.

If the market trend is down you will see wave patterns of five down and three up.

The waves are divided by different sizes. Grand Supercycle (decades), Supercycle (years), Cycle (year), Primary (months), Intermediate (month), Minor (days), Minute (day), Minuette (hours), Sub-Minuette (60 minutes or less). The waves overlay themselves but still keep the 5/3 pattern.

Variations of Impulsive Waves

There are varieties in the impulsive waves:
sometimes the 1 or 3 or 5 waves are extended.

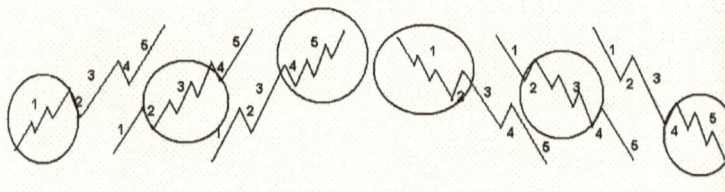

Bull   Bear

In each of these charts one of the waves that
are going with the trend is extended, meaning
that it is subdivided in another pattern of five
waves within itself. Please study the circles.

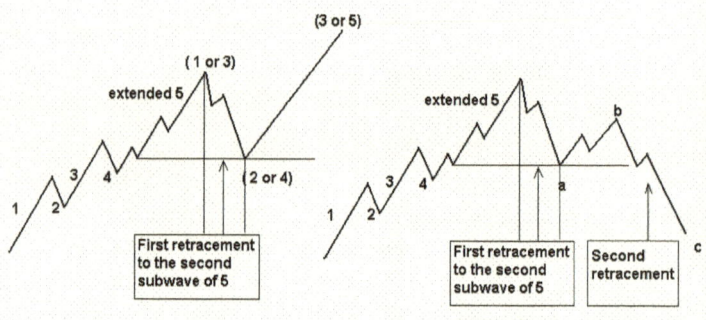

An impulsive wave can end with a single or
double retracement. Depending on the kind of
retracement the pattern can either be a
further sub-division as shown in the chart
located on the left or it is a real retracement

resulting in a corrective wave as shown in the chart located on the right.

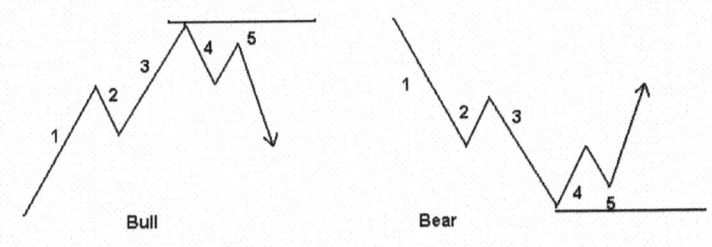

The fifth wave can fail to exceed the third, this is called a failure.

Diagonal triangles appear in the fifth wave usually when the movement has gone too far too fast.

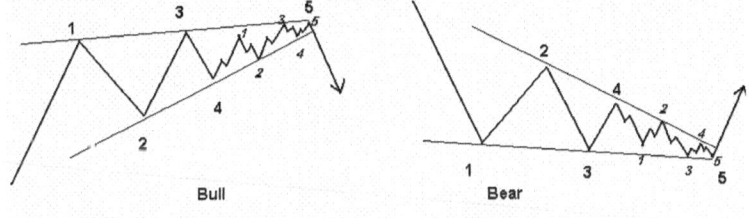

The fifth wave in a diagonal triangle usually is subdivided as shown above.

Variations of Corrective Waves (Bull-Market)

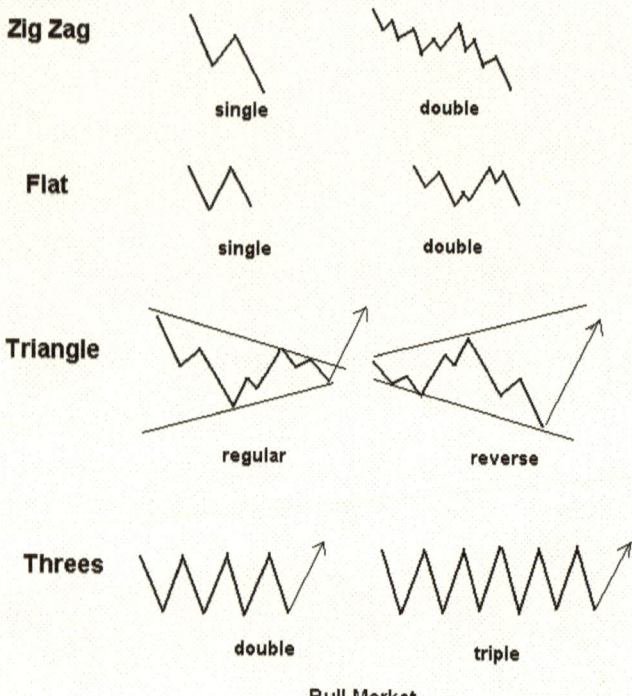

Zig Zag

single   double

Flat

single   double

Triangle

regular   reverse

Threes

double   triple

Bull-Market

Variations of Corrective Waves (Bear-Market)

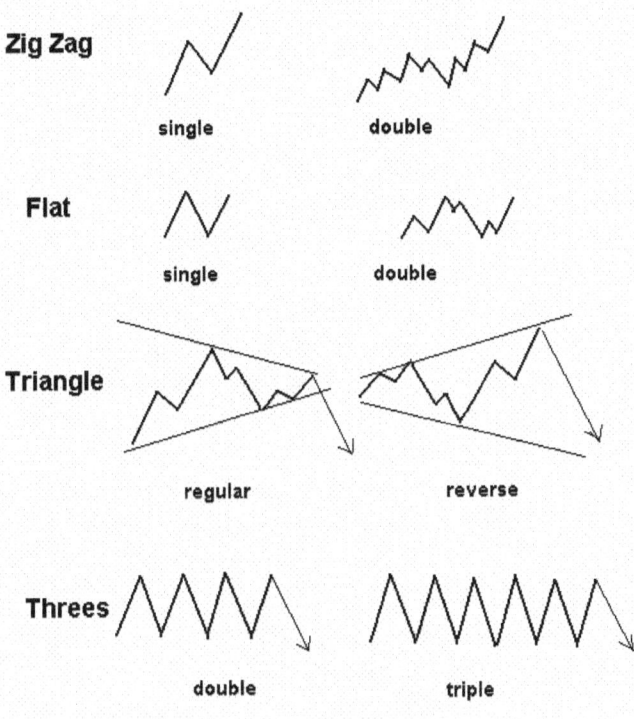

Zig Zag

single   double

Flat

single   double

Triangle

regular   reverse

Threes

double   triple

Bear-Market

Wave Personalities

In order to interpret charts more efficiently it is important to understand the following rules:

Impulsive Waves:
Impulsive Waves are **always** five – Corrective Waves can **never** be five
50 % of the time First Waves are fully taken out by the Second Wave.
Third Waves are usually the strongest with the largest volume and movement in price.
Third Waves can never be the shortest.
Fourth Waves are predictable to their extent. Their profile is often times very complex.
Fifth Waves are often smaller than popular conception holds (Don't be too greedy).

Corrective Waves:
Corrective Waves are **always** three – Impulsive Waves can **never** be three
A-Waves in Bear Markets make investors look for LONG positions.
Flat A-Waves proceed Zigzag B-Waves – Zigzag A-Waves proceed Flat B-Waves.
Upward B-Waves are often times head fakes to be fully taken out by the C-Wave.

McClellan Oscillator

The McClellan Oscillator monitors the short-term momentum of the NYSE. It does this by taking into account the advanced decline ratio as well as the fluctuating volume of stocks traded.

An oscillator by definition always oscillates around a zero line. The McClellan Oscillation in particular shows that money is moving into the market when it is above zero and money is moving out of the market when it is below zero. Readings above plus 100 mean that the market is currently overbought and therefore likely to go back down. Readings in excess of minus 100 indicate an oversold market with prices likely to rise.

It is the nature of the McClellan Oscillator to not stay above plus 100 or below minus 100 for long periods of time. The empirical conclusion is that the market will reverse its direction rather rapidly from any of these extremes.

It is not recommended to solely trade using the McClellan Oscillator as the only indicator to enter into a trade. By trying to pick the exact top or bottom of this Oscillator greed could turn into embarrassment. In conjunction with correct charting however, the McClellan Oscillator can be a helpful forecasting tool.

2. Glossary

American Depositary Receipt (ADR): A stock of a foreign company that is available for trading on US Stock Exchanges. Depositary Receipt refers to the fact that this foreign stock has to be held by a US bank representing the foreign company within the United States.

American Stock Exchange (AMEX): The second-largest stock exchange in the U.S., after NYSE. Stocks, bonds and options are traded on the AMEX.

Arbitrage: When a trader purchases a security and then sells it to someone else making a profit off from the different prices. For example: Buying a soda from the store for $1 knowing already that you can sell it immediately for $1.25.

Bear: A trader who sells or shorts stock with the intent or chance that he will buy it back at a lower price. This trader believes in falling prices.

Bear Market: When the prices within the market are decreasing. E.g.: an arena for the bear.

Bid/Ask: Just like currencies, stocks are sold to an individual trader for a higher price than he is able to sell them to an institution. The Bid is the lower price, the Ask is the higher price, the difference between the two is the spread. On high volume trading NASDAQ stocks the spread usually is no more than 1/16 exception: often times Internet stocks are traded with a considerably higher spread. Be aware that if you SOES in at Market Price (Ask) you can already be down in your position because the Bid maybe for example ½ dollar lower.

Block Trade: Is a transaction that involves over 10,000 shares or more.

Breakout: When a security breaks through a *resistance or support line* to establish a new short term high or low

Broker - The person or company that provides the trader with the means to buy and sell stocks. Typically brokers require a certain minimum of investment income as well as charge a transaction fee for each exchange.

Bug: The bug is displayed in the lower right-hand corner of CNBC. It informs the public about the DOW, NASDAQ Composite, and S&P 500 Index

Bull: A trader who buys stock with the intent or chance that he will sell them for a higher price. Trader who believes in a rise of the market.

Bull Market: When the prices within the market are rising.

Buying Power: The buying power depends on the size of the trader's account usually the buying power is twice the cash balance of the trading account. The buying power can be raised please refer to *Margin Call*.

Capitalism: Economic system in which private ownership, free competition and free markets and prices are present.

Close Position: You have completed the trade. You have closed that transaction for a profit or loss.

Daily High/ Low: The highest and lowest price a security reaches during one particular market session.

Commission: The fee charged by a brokerage for its service in facilitating the traders transactions.

Consumer Price Index (CPI): Also called cost-of-living index. A basket of products and services including: food, electricity, housing, and transportation. The CPI is published monthly. This index is one of the most feared in the market. On its release day the stock market often times shows a heavy reaction to the new number.

Day Trader: A stock trader who holds positions for a short period of time (during the same trading day) and makes multiple trades during the market session.

Depth: The number of shares that can be bought or sold in a particular stock without influencing its price.

Downtick: When the price for which a stock transaction is completed is lower than the preceding one.

Downtick Rule: In order to prevent the market from crashing NASDAQ introduced the Downtick Rule. When a stock is down-ticking (usually shown by a red down arrow in the order book) a short order can only be placed at the Ask or higher. This slows down the downdraft of the stock and prevents a lot of traders from successfully opening a short position.

Dow Jones Industrial Average: The most famous market indicator in the world. It averages 30 major stocks of the American Stock Market to determine the health of the market. Even though it only monitors 30 stocks the psychological impact on the market is great.

Earnings Report: Typically each company announces its quarterly results during the earnings season four times a year. This is done after the market closes. The released number will always be compared with the forecast and expectations the investors had. Based on this comparison the stock price could jump rather quickly up or down.

Electronic Communication Network (ECN): Allows you to be a "market maker". You can enter your order to bid or ask for a certain stock on the ECN to be displayed nation-wide. In the order book ECNs can be recognized by their 4 digit symbol. Some examples of ECNs are The ISLD, ARCA, ATTN, and others. The first ECN was INCA, Instinet, founded in 1969 for institutional trade.

FDIC: Federal Deposit Insurance Corporation; a government organization with the purpose to protect investors from bankruptcy of financial institutions in the USA.

Federal Reserve Bank: Is a governmental institution. The Fed is the guardian of the US Dollar and controls the change of interest rates. The chairman, currently Alan Greenspan, is believed to be the most influential man in the money business. Through several reports and public appearances each year he shares his thoughts about the economical well-being of the nation with the markets. In the past single statements had the power to move the stock markets up or down several percentage points within a few minutes.

FIFO: First In First Out, when a trader enters into several positions of one stock, the first position will be the first one to be closed once he starts closing his positions. The opposite is *LIFO.*

Fair Value: Is the proper relationship between the Future and the Cash. The formula for Fair Value uses short-term interest rates, amount of time left until expiration, and the current cash.

Gap: When a market or security opens significantly higher (gap up) or lower (gap down) than it closed yesterday

Golden Cross: When a fast moving average is about to cross the slower moving average on the same stock chart. Often times the stock will make a substantial move into the direction the fast moving average is headed.

Head Fakes: A situation in which Market Makers deliberately try to give you a lead into the wrong direction. Once you follow that lead they immediately display their true intentions and take full advantage of the situation.

High: Reflects the highest price of the stock for the daily, 52 week, or the all time high.

High Volume Stock: Stocks that have many shares traded per day. There are many buyers and sellers for the stock.

Instinet (INCA): The first ECN for institutions to display bids and offers on NYSE and NASDAQ. It is the most important ECN for after hours trading. Market Makers use it either to broadcast block trades to their peers or to hide the fact that they support or dump a certain stock. For example: If GSCO (Goldman Sachs) wants to drive the price of a stock up without anyone noticing that it is him, he could place his orders through INCA so that in the order book the symbol INCA appears instead of GSCO. Selected brokerage firms for day trading offer day traders access to INCA either directly or through a master terminal.

IPO: Initial Public Offering: The debut of a stock on a stock exchange.

Island (ISLD): *Electronic Communication Network (ECN)* The Island Book is currently the most liquid of all ECN's. It is owned by DATEK.

Level II: When using Level II experienced traders can actually see all of the bid and ask prices as well as the Market Makers who displaying them. Level II shows the name of the market maker by their 4 digit ticker symbol. Items in yellow show the market makers with the best bid or ask prices. Items in green are the second best, blue are the third best, red are the fourth best and so on. The left side is the bid and the right side is the ask. When using the first level, traders only see the first bid/ask level which would indicate that the stock is about to go down (because it is 12/20). As you see in the example below the market makers on the left side shown in yellow add up to 62 and the market makers on the right side shown in yellow is 20. This means that the demand is far more than what it seemed using Level I. Level II displays when the bid or ask has been filled. If GSCO sells its 20,000 shares he will be out of shares and no longer appear on the screen.

If a market maker really wants the stock he can raise the amount of which he is willing to buy. If PRUS really would like these shares he can raise the bid price above 18 ¼ . PRUS would than move to the top of the list above MLCO and LEHM.

Name	Bid	Size	Name	Ask	Size
MLCO	18 1/4	12	GSCO	18 3/8	20
LEHM	18 1/4	20	MASH	18 1/2	10
PRUS	18 1/4	30	AGED	18 5/8	17
BEST	18 1/8	10	SHWD	18 5/8	10
TSCO	18 1/16	10	TSCO	18 3/4	50

LIFO: Last In First Out When a trader enters several positions of a stock, the last opened position will be the first to be closed once he decides to close his positions. The opposite of this is *FIFO*.

Limit Order: An order that limits the price at which the order is executed. For example: Limit buy Microsoft 90 means that buy Microsoft at $ 90 or less not just at the market price. The market price could be higher.

Limit Down: Indices and futures are protected from falling too deep by enforcing limit rules for negative market trends. When the S&P Future for example hits limit down, being X points below yesterday's close. For the next 15 minutes the Futures can only trade at the same price or higher. After the 15 minutes the Futures could drop to the next Limit Line. The Dow Jones Limits are imposed as trading curbs. Once the Dow Jones drops more than 2% below yesterday's close "Curbs are in Effect" meaning that all electronic trading is suspended until the curbs are lifted. The easiest way to detect a curb is watching the Dow Jones Bug on CNBC a red notice "Curbs In" will be shown. Although big movements like these do not regularly occur it is possible that an ongoing decrease of the price can cause the market to be halted and therefore the index being limit locked. Trading will then begin after 30 minutes or even the next trading day because market regulators assume that the over-heated reactions have calmed down by then. These rules are imposed to protect investors of all sizes from market crashes like in 1929.

Liquidity: The volume that is traded in a particular security. Day traders always look for liquid stocks in order to be able to get in and out quickly.

Long: Buy a stock with the intention to sell later at a higher price – the risk potential of a long is limited to the amount of money you paid for the position.

Low: Reflects the lowest price of the stock during the daily, 52 week, or the all time low.

Market Order : An order to buy or sell at the current market price which is not always the best price.

Maintenance Call: Even though it is the goal of pure day trading to be all in cash overnight, a trader might hold positions for several days. Each position is required to be covered with cash in case that the trader holds too many positions or holds positions that turn against him. The funds in his account might not be enough to cover these trades. Securities regulations require that a trader has to prove that he actually would have had the money to cover his positions. Since the positions are still open the money actually has to stay in the account until either the positions are closed or they have turned profitable. A broker will inform his trader about a maintenance call usually 3-5 days before the trader has to meet this call. Failure to meet the call will result in mandatory closing of as many positions necessary to cover the call.

Margin Call: During any given time of the market session a trader is allowed to hold stock in the value of twice his account balance. This is known as buying power. If the trader exceeds this limit and uses more money than he is trading on margin. Securities regulations require that a trader has to prove that he actually would have had the money to cover his transactions even though he might have closed all of his positions at the end of the market session. Therefore the broker will inform his trader that he has to transfer money into the account to cover his trades. Since the trades are already closed the money only has to be there for one day provided that the trader does not exceed his buying power again.

Market Maker: Institutional broker on NASDAQ with the task to provide liquidity and fair pricing for stocks. In contrast to NYSE, Market Maker's on NASDAQ are not assigned to service a particular stock. Here are some of the more dominant Market Makers and their order book symbols: Goldman Sachs (GSCO), Merrill Lynch (MLCO), Morgan Stanley (MSCO), Spear Leeds and Kellogg (SPLK), and Herzog (HRZG)

Market Trend: The direction of the market either in an upward or downward movement.

NYSE: The New York Stock Exchange is the largest stock exchange in the world. It is a true stock exchange in the sense of how trades are handled. Each listed stock managed by a particular specialist who ensures that stock is traded at a fair price in regards to supply and demand. Every trade has to go through the specialist for that particular stock. Listed NYSE stocks have 1-3 digit ticker symbols. For example T is AT&T, GE is General Electric, and MOT is Motorola.

NASDAQ: The largest electronic stock exchange in the world. All trades are matched through a computer system. There are no specialists on NASDAQ – Market Makers have to ensure decent pricing. Typically each stock is being traded by several Market Makers. A day trader who uses an *ECN (Electronic Communication Network)* can act as a "Market Maker" himself. This market is faster to trade in because it is electronic. All the trades are completed directly through the computer, a stock exchange like this is known as an OTC or Over-The-Counter Market. Each stock on NASDAQ has a Ticker Symbol with either 4 or 5 digits. For example MSFT is Microsoft and ERICY is Ericsson (Ericsson is a foreign company as indicated by the Y at the end of the ticker. *See ADR for more information*).

NASDAQ Composite: Is a market weighted index of all listed stocks on NASDAQ (the biggest stock has the highest impact on the market movement currently the biggest stock is Microsoft).

Open Position: The trader is in a trade (either long or short) and it is not closed out yet. Until he closes that position the profit or loss is not realized.

Reg. FD: *SEC* **R**egulation about **F**ull **D**isclosure of important company information to the public

Russell 2000 index: Index of 2000 small capital stocks

Scalp: A quick trade, executed within seconds, usually to gain a small percentage amount of the stock value.

SEC: Security and Exchange Commission; the governmental regulatory agency to oversee financial institutions.

Selectnet (order): Gives traders the opportunity to negotiate the price through NASDAQ with one particular Market Maker. For example: Selectnet Preference: SelectnetBuy 200 MSFT at $ 90 from GSCO. This is a bid directly to Goldman Sachs none of the other Market Makers can see it.   You can also bid to all of the Market Makers who show at a particular price level. For example: Selectnet Order: SelectnetBuy 200 MSFT at $ 90. A Selectnet order once entered cannot be cancelled during the first 10 seconds!

Sell-off: A sudden drop of the market in reaction to economic news. For example: in the middle of trading the Federal Reserve announces an unexpected raise in interest Rates which causes the market to turn down sharply.

Short: The trader has sold stock he does not yet own. He will have to buy the stock back at a later time in order to complete that trade. When a trader sells something he doesn't have he is "short". This is the second way for traders to make money. If the trader believes that the price of a stock will decrease he can choose to sell it at the current price (even though he does not yet own it), then when the price does decline he purchases the stock for a lower price. Even if the stock price rises and this trade becomes non-profitable he must buy back the stock to close his position. Typically trading short is done on a short-term basis. Be aware that the risk potential of a short is unlimited.

SIPC: Securities Investors Protection Corporation; an organization formed with the purpose to protect investors against financial default of member financial institutions.

Split: An increase in the number of outstanding shares of a particular company. It usually occurs once the stock has hit a certain price level. If the stock is too expensive, it will not be traded as active as before. Therefore the company decides to split one share for example into two new shares. The overall value of the company is not affected by the changes. For example, after a 2 for 1 split there are twice as many shares. But these shares will only be half of the price.

Specialist: In opposition to the electronic matching of orders on NASDAQ the NYSE still operates widely with manual matching of orders. The specialist records all open orders and builds the price for a stock at which most trades can be executed. Each specialist is responsible for certain stocks.

Stock: A financial instrument used to claim ownership or equity in a corporation.

The Stock Market: The trading of stocks in an organized environment known as exchange.

SOES: Small Order Execution System The trader always buys on the offer and sells on the bid to a Market Maker. Orders are executed on a first come first serve basis yet they are executed automatically. Market Makers who show up on the offer or bid of the particular stock are obligated to honor all orders within the maximum of the SOES share size limits. For each stock there is a limit for the maximum number of shares that can be executed in a single trade via SOES. This can be for example 200, 500, or 1,000 shares. In the order book this number is displayed by SM2, SM5, or SM10. With the introduction of Super-SOES, individuals can now execute trades of up to 9,999 shares in this System. The system has recently been updated and is also referred to as Super-Montage now.

Standard & Poor's 500 (S&P 500): The most commonly used indicator of market direction. The S&P 500 analyzes a broad base of 500 stocks in a variety of industries.

Technical Analysis: The analysis of a stock's future based strictly on the numbers. For example: earnings, sales, and assets.

30 Year Bond: When the bond prices rise there is a decrease in the yields people receive from them. When people are not making as much money investing in bonds they will invest more in the stock market. So when Bond interest rates are low more people will invest in the Stock Market, when they are high investors will move money from the Stock Market to Bonds.

Ticker: A horizontal display that usually scrolls form right to left displaying a certain stock, its actual price and the amount of shares traded for that price at this particular trade. Stocks that are shown in red are negative for the day. Stocks shown in green are positive for the day.

Stocks that are shown in blue have not changed. A ticker could also display indices or bonds and futures.

Trade: A completed transaction of entering and exiting into a stock position. For Example: Buy 500 shares of MSFT then sell 500 shares of MSFT. At the end of the trade the trader has realized either a profit or a loss.

Trading Range: The price range in which a particular security usually trades.

YTD: Year To Date is the period of time between a particular day during the year and January 1st of that same year.

52 week high /low: the highest or lowest price a particular stock reached during the last 52weeks